Spiritual Life Songs

HARRY P. ARMSTRONG, Music Editor

D1316235

ISBN 0-687-39228-4

Abingdon Press

06 07—64 63 62

FOREWORD

There is no part of public worship which calls for more serious and intelligent consideration than the selection of hymns suited to the occasion and to the congregation.

In this collection of *Spiritual Life Songs* the editors have assembled one hundred and forty-two of the best hymns of the Church. Through them the majestic voice of the Christian centuries is heard. They preserve the distinctly evangelical note of Protestantism. They express our devout and fervent spirit of worship, as well as the ever-recurring insistence upon a vital Christian experience and lives of Christlike service. Here are hymns for the penitent, the "backslider," and the victorious believer.

Spiritual Life Songs represent the careful work of an able editorial group commissioned to select the choice numbers from the best songbook publishers of the world. A good many of the songs were obtained at an expense not ordinarily involved in a small songbook.

In no way is this book planned to compete with the denominational church hymnals. It aims simply to provide a serviceable, inexpensive collection of familiar hymns and songs for use in special meetings and other religious gatherings which usually require a small book of this type.

The Publishers earnestly hope that the worshipful use of this book will quicken the spiritual life of all who sing from it.

THE PUBLISHERS.

1   Doxology

THOS. KEN

G. FRANC

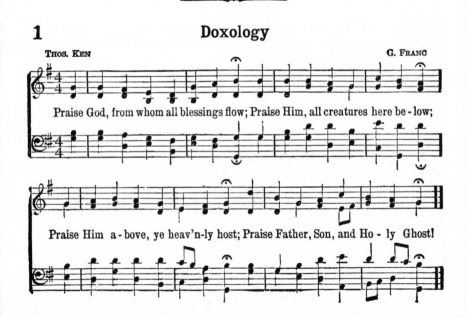

Praise God, from whom all blessings flow; Praise Him, all creatures here be-low;

Praise Him a-bove, ye heav'n-ly host; Praise Father, Son, and Ho-ly Ghost!

SPIRITUAL LIFE SONGS

2

O Worship The King

Sir Robert Grant

Francis Joseph Haydn

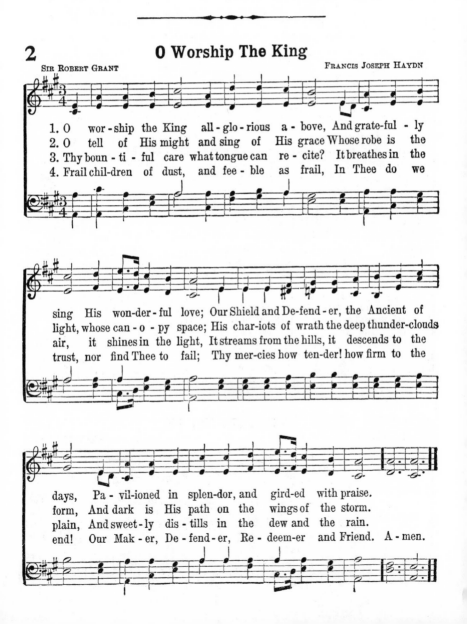

1. O wor-ship the King all-glo-rious a-bove, And grate-ful-ly
sing His won-der-ful love; Our Shield and De-fend-er, the Ancient of
days, Pa-vil-ioned in splen-dor, and gird-ed with praise.

2. O tell of His might and sing of His grace Whose robe is the
light, whose can-o-py space; His char-iots of wrath the deep thunder-clouds
form, And dark is His path on the wings of the storm.

3. Thy boun-ti-ful care what tongue can re-cite? It breathes in the
air, it shines in the light, It streams from the hills, it descends to the
plain, And sweet-ly dis-tills in the dew and the rain.

4. Frail chil-dren of dust, and fee-ble as frail, In Thee do we
trust, nor find Thee to fail; Thy mer-cies how ten-der! how firm to the
end! Our Mak-er, De-fend-er, Re-deem-er and Friend. A-men.

3 All Hail the Power of Jesus' Name

EDWARD PERRONET

OLIVER HOLDEN

1. All hail the pow'r of Je-sus' name, Let an-gels pros-trate fall;
2. Crown Him, ye morn-ing stars of light, Who fixed this earth-ly ball;
3. Sin-ners, whose love can ne'er for-get The wormwood and the gall,
4. Let ev-'ry kin-dred, ev-'ry tribe, On this ter-res-trial ball,
5. O that with yon-der sa-cred throng We at His feet may fall;

Bring forth the roy-al di-a-dem, And crown Him Lord of all,
Now hail the strength of Is-rael's might, And crown Him Lord of all,
Go, spread your tro-phies at His feet, And crown Him Lord of all,
To Him all maj-es-ty as-cribe, And crown Him Lord of all,
We'll join the ev-er-last-ing song, And crown Him Lord of all,

Bring forth the roy-al di-a-dem, And crown Him Lord of all.
Now hail the strength of Is-rael's might, And crown Him Lord of all.
Go, spread your tro-phies at His feet, And crown Him Lord of all.
To Him all maj-es-ty as-cribe, And crown Him Lord of all.
We'll join the ev-er-last-ing song, And crown Him Lord of all.

4 Blest Be the Tie

JOHN FAWCETT

HANS G. NAEGELI

1. Blest be the tie that binds Our hearts in Chris-tian love; The
2. Be-fore our Fa-ther's throne, We pour our ar-dent prayers; Our
3. We share our mu-tual woes, Our mu-tual bur-dens bear; And
4. When we a-sun-der part, It gives us in-ward pain; But

Blest Be the Tie

fel - low - ship of kin - dred minds Is like to that a - bove.
fears, our hopes, our aims are one, Our com - forts and our cares.
oft - en for each oth - er flows The sym - pa - thiz - ing tear.
we shall still be joined in heart, And hope to meet a - gain.

5 There is a Fountain

WILLIAM COWPER   LOWELL MASON

1. There is a foun-tain filled with blood Drawn from Im - man - uel's veins;
2. The dy - ing thief re - joiced to see That foun - tain in his day;
3. Dear dy - ing Lamb, Thy pre-cious blood Shall nev - er lose its pow'r,
4. E'er since, by faith, I saw the stream Thy flow - ing wounds sup - ply,
5. Then in a no - bler, sweet-er song, I'll sing Thy pow'r to save,

FINE

D.S.-And sin-ners, plunged be-neath that flood, Lose all their guilt - y stains.
D.S.-And there may I, though vile as he, Wash all my sins a - way.
D.S.-Till all the ran-somed church of God Be saved, to sin no more.
D.S.-Re - deem-ing love has been my theme, And shall be till I die.
D.S.-When this poor lisp-ing, stamm'ring tongue Lies si - lent in the grave.

D. S.

Lose all their guilt - y stains,   Lose all their guilt - y stains;
Wash all my sins a - way,   Wash all my sins a - way;
Be saved, to sin no more,   Be saved, to sin no more;
And shall be till I die,   And shall be till I die;
Lies si - lent in the grave,   Lies si - lent in the grave;

6 In The Cross Of Christ

SIR JOHN BOWRING

ITHAMAR CONKEY

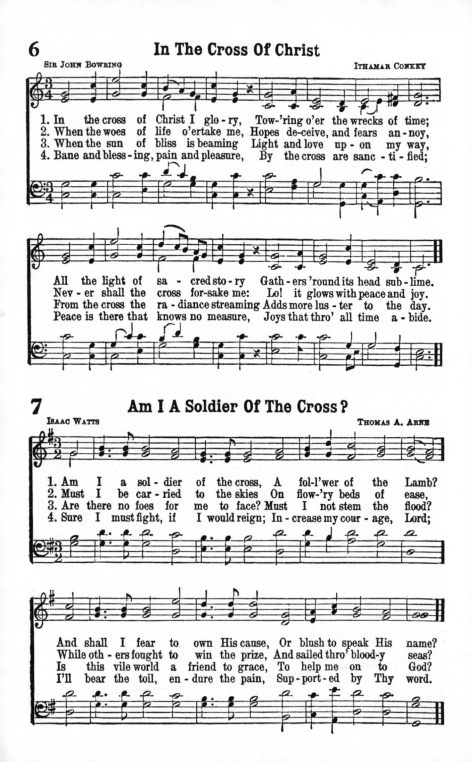

1. In the cross of Christ I glo - ry, Tow-'ring o'er the wrecks of time;
2. When the woes of life o'ertake me, Hopes de-ceive, and fears an - noy,
3. When the sun of bliss is beaming Light and love up - on my way,
4. Bane and bless - ing, pain and pleasure, By the cross are sanc - ti - fied;

All the light of sa - cred sto - ry Gath-ers 'round its head sub - lime.
Nev - er shall the cross for-sake me: Lo! it glows with peace and joy.
From the cross the ra - diance streaming Adds more lus - ter to the day.
Peace is there that knows no measure, Joys that thro' all time a - bide.

7 Am I A Soldier Of The Cross?

ISAAC WATTS

THOMAS A. ARNE

1. Am I a sol - dier of the cross, A fol-l'wer of the Lamb?
2. Must I be car - ried to the skies On flow-'ry beds of ease,
3. Are there no foes for me to face? Must I not stem the flood?
4. Sure I must fight, if I would reign; In - crease my cour - age, Lord;

And shall I fear to own His cause, Or blush to speak His name?
While oth - ers fought to win the prize, And sailed thro' blood-y seas?
Is this vile world a friend to grace, To help me on to God?
I'll bear the toil, en - dure the pain, Sup-port-ed by Thy word.

8   Onward, Christian Soldiers

SABINE BARING-GOULD   ARTHUR SULLIVAN

1. On-ward, Christian sol - diers! Marching as to war, With the cross of
2. Like a might-y ar - my Moves the Church of God; Brothers, we are
3. Crowns and thrones may per-ish, Kingdoms rise and wane; But the Church of
4. On-ward, then, ye peo - ple! Join our happy throng; Blend with ours your

Je - sus Go - ing on be - fore; Christ, the roy - al Mas - ter,
tread - ing Where the saints have trod; We are not di - vid - ed,
Je - sus Con-stant will re - main; Gates of hell can nev - er
voic - es In the tri-umph song; Glo - ry, laud, and hon - or,

Leads a-gainst the foe; For-ward in - to bat - tle, See, His banners go!
All one bod - y we; One in hope and doc - trine, One in char - i - ty.
'Gainst that Church prevail; We have Christ's own promise, Which can never fail.
Un - to Christ the King; This thro' countless a - ges Men and an - gels sing.

CHORUS

On-ward, Chris-tian sol - diers! March-ing as to war,

With the cross of Je - sus Go - ing on be - fore.

Faith of Our Fathers

FREDERICK W. FABER

H. F. HEMY

1. Faith of our fa - thers! liv - ing still In spite of dun-geon, fire and sword:
2. Our fa-thers, chained in prisons dark, Were still in heart and conscience free:
3. Faith of our fa - thers! we will love Both friend and foe in all our strife:

O how our hearts beat high with joy Whene'er we hear that glo-rious word!
How sweet would be their children's fate, If they, like them, could die for thee!
And preach thee, too, as love knows how, By kind-ly words and vir-tuous life:

Faith of our fa-thers! ho - ly faith! We will be true to thee till death!
Faith of our fa-thers! ho - ly faith! We will be true to thee till death!
Faith of our fa-thers! ho - ly faith! We will be true to thee till death!

10 Holy Ghost, with Light Divine

A. REED

GOTTSCHALK

1. Ho - ly Ghost, with light di - vine, Shine up - on this heart of mine;
2. Ho - ly Ghost, with pow'r di - vine, Cleanse this guilt-y heart of mine;
3. Ho - ly Ghost, with joy di - vine, Cheer this saddened heart of mine;
4. Ho - ly Spir - it, all di - vine, Dwell with-in this heart of mine;

Holy Ghost, with Light Divine

Chase the shades of night a - way, Turn my dark-ness in - to day.
Long hath sin with-out con-trol, Held do - min-ion o'er my soul.
Bid my man-y woes de - part, Heal my wound-ed, bleed-ing heart.
Cast down ev - 'ry i - dol throne. Reign su-preme—and reign a - lone.

11 Break Thou the Bread of Life

MARY ANN LATHBURY

WILLIAM F. SHERWIN

1. Break Thou the bread of life, Dear Lord, to me, As Thou didst
2. Bless Thou the truth, dear Lord, To me—to me— As Thou didst
3. O send Thy Spir - it, Lord, Now un - to me, That He may
4. Thou art the bread of life, O Lord, to me, Thy ho - ly

break the loaves Be - side the sea; Be - yond the sa - cred page
bless the bread By Gal - i - lee; Then shall all bond - age cease,
touch my eyes, And make me see: Show me the truth con-cealed
Word the truth That sav - eth me; Give me to eat and live

I seek Thee, Lord; My spir - it pants for Thee, O liv - ing Word.
All fet - ters fall; And I shall find my peace, My All in all.
With-in Thy Word, And in Thy book re-vealed I see the Lord.
With Thee a - bove; Teach me to love Thy truth, For Thou art love.

12 O Love That Wilt Not Let Me Go

GEORGE MATHESON

A. L. PEACE

1. O Love that wilt not let me go, I rest my wea - ry
2. O Light that fol - low'st all my way, I yield my flick - 'ring
3. O Joy that seek - est me thro' pain, I can - not close my
4. O Cross that lift - est up my head, I dare not ask to

soul in Thee; I give Thee back the life I owe, That
torch to Thee; My heart re - stores its bor - rowed ray, That
heart to Thee; I trace the rain - bow thro' the rain, And
hide from Thee; I lay in dust life's glo - ry dead, And

in Thine o - cean depths its flow May rich - er, full - er be.
in Thy sun - shine's glow its day May bright - er, fair - er be.
feel the prom - ise is not vain That morn shall tear - less be.
from the ground there blossoms red Life that shall end - less be.

13 On Jordan's Stormy Banks

SAMUEL STENNETT

Arr. by R. M. McINTOSH

1. On Jor - dan's stormy banks I stand, And cast a wish - ful eye
2. All o'er those wide, ex - tend - ed plains Shines one e - ter - nal day;
3. No chill - ing winds, nor pois'nous breath, Can reach that healthful shore;
4. When shall I reach that hap - py place, And be for - ev - er blest?

On Jordan's Stormy Banks

FINE.

To Ca-naan's fair and hap-py land, Where my pos-ses-sions lie.
There God, the Son, for-ev-er reigns, And scat-ters night a-way.
Sick-ness and sor-row, pain and death, Are felt and feared no more.
When shall I see my Fa-ther's face, And in His bos-om rest?

D. S.—O who will come and go with me? I am bound for the promised land.

REFRAIN

D. S.

I am bound for the promised land,...... I am bound for the promised land.
promised land,

---

14 ## Come, Thou Fount

ROBERT ROBINSON

JOHN WYETH
FINE.

1. {Come, Thou Fount of ev-'ry bless-ing, Tune my heart to sing Thy grace;}
   {Streams of mer-cy, nev-er ceas-ing, Call for songs of loud-est praise.}

2. {Here I'll raise my Eb-en-e-zer, Hith-er by Thy help I'll come;}
   {And I hope, by Thy good pleasure, Safe-ly to ar-rive at home.}

3. {Oh, to grace How great a debt-or Dai-ly I'm constrained to be!}
   {Let Thy good-ness, like a fet-ter, Bind my trust-ing heart to Thee:}

D.C.—Praise the mount, I'm fixed up-on it! Mount of Thy re-deem-ing love.
D.C.—He, to res-cue me from dan-ger, In-ter-posed His pre-cious blood.
D.C.—Here's my heart, O take and seal it, Seal it for Thy courts a-bove.

D. C.

Teach me some me-lo-dious son-net, Sung by flam-ing tongues a-bove;
Je-sus sought me when a stran-ger, Wand'ring from the fold of God;
Prone to wan-der, Lord, I feel it, Prone to leave the God I love;

15 Day Is Dying In The West

MARY A. LATHBURY

WILLIAM F. SHERWIN

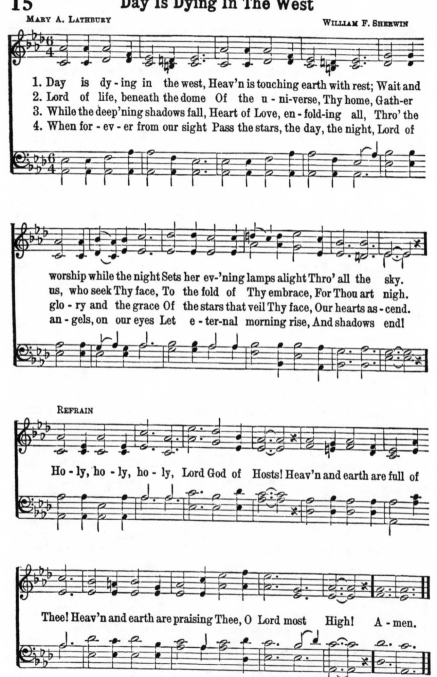

1. Day is dy-ing in the west, Heav'n is touching earth with rest; Wait and
2. Lord of life, beneath the dome Of the u-ni-verse, Thy home, Gath-er
3. While the deep'ning shadows fall, Heart of Love, en-fold-ing all, Thro' the
4. When for-ev-er from our sight Pass the stars, the day, the night, Lord of

worship while the night Sets her ev-'ning lamps alight Thro' all the sky.
us, who seek Thy face, To the fold of Thy embrace, For Thou art nigh.
glo-ry and the grace Of the stars that veil Thy face, Our hearts as-cend.
an-gels, on our eyes Let e-ter-nal morning rise, And shadows end!

REFRAIN

Ho-ly, ho-ly, ho-ly, Lord God of Hosts! Heav'n and earth are full of

Thee! Heav'n and earth are praising Thee, O Lord most High! A-men.

He Leadeth Me

JOSEPH H. GILMORE

WILLIAM B. BRADBURY

1. He lead-eth me! O bless-ed tho't! O words with heav'nly comfort fraught!
2. Sometimes 'mid scenes of deepest gloom, Some-times where E-den's bowers bloom,
3. Lord, I would clasp Thy hand in mine, Nor ev-er mur-mur nor re-pine,
4. And when my task on earth is done, When, by Thy grace, the vic-t'ry's won,

What-e'er I do, wher-e'er I be, Still 'tis God's hand that lead-eth me.
By wa-ters still, o'er troub-led sea,— Still 'tis His hand that lead-eth me!
Con-tent, what-ev-er lot I see, Since 'tis my God that lead-eth me!
E'en death's cold wave I will not flee, Since God thro' Jor-dan lead-eth me.

REFRAIN

He lead-eth me, He lead-eth me, By His own hand He lead-eth me:

His faith-ful fol-lower I would be, For by His hand He lead-eth me.

17 Amazing Grace

JOHN NEWTON

1. A - maz-ing grace! how sweet the sound, That saved a wretch like me! I
2. 'Twas grace that taught my heart to fear, And grace my fears re-lieved; How
3. Thro' man - y dan-gers, toils and snares, I have al - read - y come; 'Tis
4. When we've been there ten thousand years, Bright shining as the sun, We've

once was lost, but now am found, Was blind, but now I see.
pre - cious did that grace ap-pear The hour I first be-lieved!
grace hath bro't me safe thus far, And grace will lead me home.
no less days to sing God's praise Than when we first be - gun. A-men.

18 Loving Kindness

SAMUEL MEDLEY   L. M.   WILLIAM CALDWELL

1. A - wake, my soul, to joy - ful lays, And sing thy great Redeemer's praise;
2. He saw me ru - ined by the fall, Yet loved me, not-with-stand-ing all;
3. Tho' num'rous hosts of might-y foes, Tho' earth and hell my way op-pose,
4. When trouble, like a gloom-y cloud, Has gathered thick and thundered loud,

He just - ly claims a song from me: His lov - ing kind - ness, O how free!
He saved me from my lost es - tate: His lov - ing kind - ness, O how great!
He safe - ly leads my soul a - long: His lov - ing kind - ness, O how strong!
He near my soul has al-ways stood: His lov - ing kind - ness, O how good!

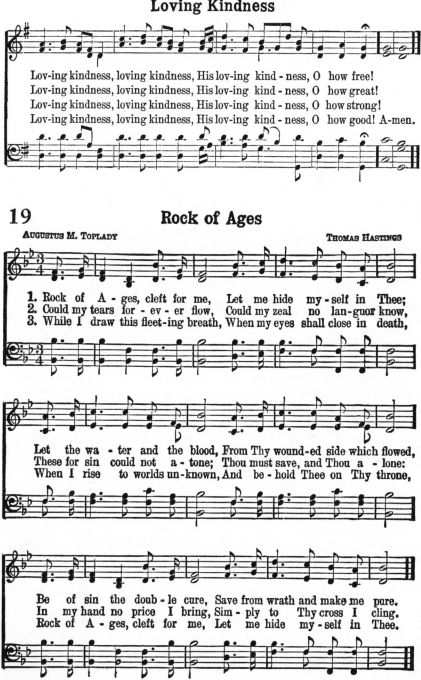

Lov-ing kindness, loving kindness, His lov-ing kind - ness, O how free!
Lov-ing kindness, loving kindness, His lov-ing kind - ness, O how great!
Lov-ing kindness, loving kindness, His lov-ing kind - ness, O how strong!
Lov-ing kindness, loving kindness, His lov-ing kind - ness, O how good! A-men.

19   **Rock of Ages**

AUGUSTUS M. TOPLADY   THOMAS HASTINGS

1. Rock of A - ges, cleft for me, Let me hide my - self in Thee;
2. Could my tears for - ev - er flow, Could my zeal no lan-guor know,
3. While I draw this fleet-ing breath, When my eyes shall close in death,

Let the wa - ter and the blood, From Thy wound-ed side which flowed,
These for sin could not a - tone; Thou must save, and Thou a - lone:
When I rise to worlds un-known, And be - hold Thee on Thy throne,

Be of sin the doub - le cure, Save from wrath and make me pure.
In my hand no price I bring, Sim - ply to Thy cross I cling.
Rock of A - ges, cleft for me, Let me hide my - self in Thee.

Take Time to Be Holy

W. D. LONGSTAFF

GEO. C. STEBBINS

1. Take time to be ho - ly, Speak oft with thy Lord; A - bide in Him
2. Take time to be ho - ly, The world rush-es on;.. Spend much time in
3. Take time to be ho - ly, Let Him be thy Guide, And run not be-
4. Take time to be ho - ly, Be calm in thy soul;. Each tho't and each

al - ways, And feed on His Word. Make friends of God's chil - dren;
se - cret With Je - sus a - lone; By look - ing to Je - sus,
fore Him, What - ev - er be - tide;.. In joy or in sor - row,
mo - tive Be - neath His con - trol;.. Thus led by His Spir - it

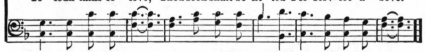

Help those who are weak; For - get-ting in noth-ing His bless-ing to seek.
Like Him thou shalt be;.. Thy friends in thy con-duct His likeness shall see;.
Still fol - low thy Lord, And, look-ing to Je - sus, Still trust in His Word.
To foun-tains of love, Thou soon shalt be fit - ted For serv-ice a - bove.

Copyright, 1918, by Geo. C. Stebbins. Renewal. Hope Publishing Company, owner

Must Jesus Bear the Cross Alone?

THOS. SHEPHERD

GEO. N. ALLEN

1. Must Je - sus bear the cross a - lone, And all the world go free?
2. How hap - py are the saints a - bove, Who once went sor-rowing here!
3. The con - se - cra - ted cross I'll bear, Till death shall set me free;
4. Up - on the crys - tal pave-ment, down, At Je - sus' pierc - ed feet,

Must Jesus Bear the Cross Alone?

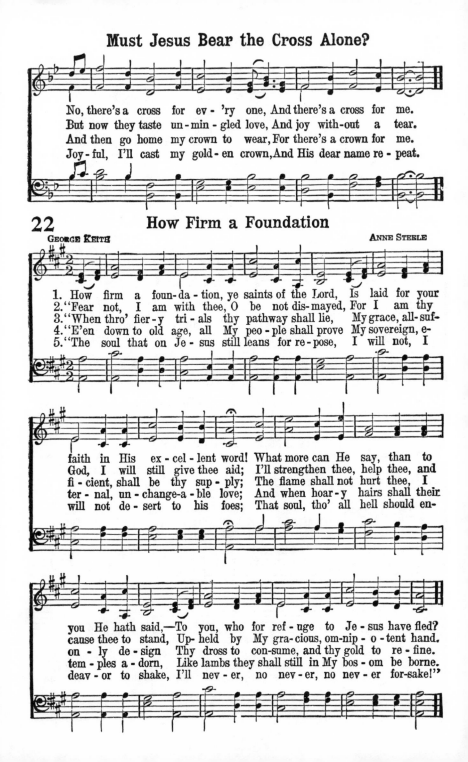

No, there's a cross for ev - 'ry one, And there's a cross for me.
But now they taste un - min - gled love, And joy with-out a tear.
And then go home my crown to wear, For there's a crown for me.
Joy - ful, I'll cast my gold - en crown, And His dear name re - peat.

22 How Firm a Foundation

GEORGE KEITH

ANNE STEELE

1. How firm a foun - da - tion, ye saints of the Lord, Is laid for your
2. "Fear not, I am with thee, O be not dis - mayed, For I am thy
3. "When thro' fier - y tri - als thy pathway shall lie, My grace, all-suf-
4. "E'en down to old age, all My peo - ple shall prove My sovereign, e-
5. "The soul that on Je - sus still leans for re - pose, I will not, I

faith in His ex - cel - lent word! What more can He say, than to
God, I will still give thee aid; I'll strengthen thee, help thee, and
fi - cient, shall be thy sup - ply; The flame shall not hurt thee, I
ter - nal, un - change-a - ble love; And when hoar - y hairs shall their
will not de - sert to his foes; That soul, tho' all hell should en-

you He hath said,—To you, who for ref - uge to Je - sus have fled?
cause thee to stand, Up - held by My gra - cious, om-nip - o - tent hand.
on - ly de - sign Thy dross to con-sume, and thy gold to re - fine.
tem - ples a - dorn, Like lambs they shall still in My bos - om be borne.
deav - or to shake, I'll nev - er, no nev - er, no nev - er for-sake!"

23 I Will Arise and Go to Jesus

J. HART

Arranged

1. Come, ye sin-ners, poor and need-y, Weak and wound-ed, sick and sore;
2. Come, ye thirst-y, come, and welcome, God's free boun-ty glo-ri-fy;
3. Come, ye wea-ry, heav-y-la-den, Lost and ru-ined by the fall;
4. Let not conscience make you lin-ger, Nor of fit-ness fond-ly dream;

CHO.—*I will a-rise and go to Je-sus, He will em-brace me in His arms;*

D. C. for Chorus

Je-sus read-y stands to save you, Full of pit-y, love and pow'r.
True be-lief and true re-pent-ance, Ev-'ry grace that brings you nigh.
If you tar-ry till you're bet-ter, You will nev-er come at all.
All the fit-ness He re-quir-eth Is to feel your need of Him.

In the arms of my dear Sav-ior, Oh, there are ten thou-sand charms.

24 My Jesus, I Love Thee

ANONYMOUS

A. J. GORDON

1. My Je-sus, I love Thee, I know Thou art mine, For Thee all the
2. I'll love Thee in life, I will love Thee in death, And praise Thee as
3. In mansions of glo-ry and end-less de-light, I'll ev-er a-

fol-lies of sin I re-sign; My gra-cious Re-deem-er, my
long as Thou lend-est me breath; And say when the death-dew lies
dore Thee in heav-en so bright; I'll sing with the glit-ter-ing

My Jesus, I Love Thee

Sav - ior art Thou; If ev - er I loved Thee, my Je - sus, 'tis now.
cold on my brow, If ev - er I loved Thee, my Je - sus, 'tis now.
crown on my brow, If ev - er I loved Thee, my Je - sus, 'tis now.

25 Jesus Calls Us

Mrs. Cecil F. Alexander

William H. Jude

1. Je - sus calls us; o'er the tu - mult Of our life's wild, rest - less sea,
2. Je - sus calls us from the wor - ship Of the vain world's gold - en store,
3. In our joys and in our sor - rows, Days of toil and hours of ease,
4. Je - sus calls us; by Thy mer - cies, Sav - ior, may we hear Thy call,

Day by day His sweet voice sound - eth, Say - ing, "Chris - tian, fol - low Me."
From each i - dol that would keep us, Say - ing, "Chris - tian, love Me more."
Still He calls, in cares and pleas - ures, "Chris - tian, love Me more than these."
Give our hearts to Thy o - be - dience, Serve and love Thee best of all.

26 His Yoke Is Easy

R. E. Hudson

His yoke is eas - y, His bur - den is light, I've found it so, I've found it so;

He lead - eth me, by day and by night, Where liv - ing wa - ters flow.

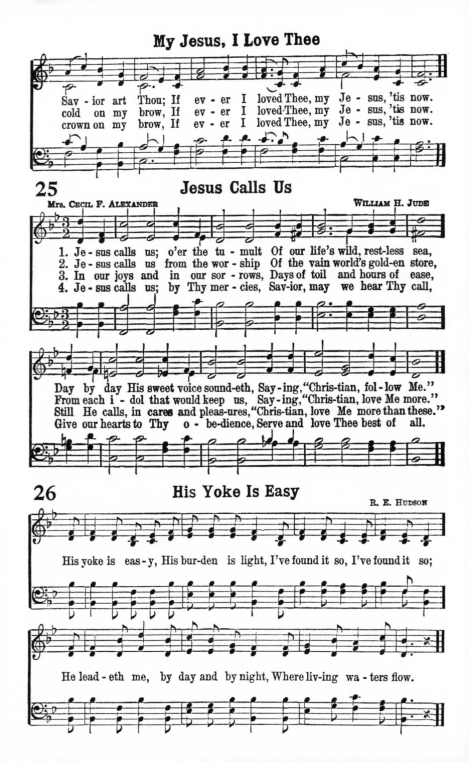

27 I Love Jesus

E. E. HEWITT

B. D. ACKLEY

Not too fast

1. I love Je - sus, for He saved my soul; From His cross the tides of
2. I love Je - sus, for He's al - ways near, Ev - er read - y with a
3. I love Je - sus when the joy-beams glow; Love Him, when the storm-y

mer - cy roll; Long and far He sought me, when a - stray;
word of cheer; Ev - 'ry day, and ev - 'ry pass - ing hour,
tem - pests blow; I will praise Him while the a - ges roll;

CHORUS.

Now, He leads me in His own right way.
I will trust Him for His keep-ing pow'r. I love Je - sus; He's my King;
Hal - le - lu - jah! for He saved my soul.

Of His mer - cy I will sing; I will fol - low in His

paths of light, Till I see Him in His glo - ry bright.

28 Ring the Bells of Heaven

W. O. Cushing

G. F. Root

Joyfully

1. Ring the bells of heav-en! there is joy to-day, For a soul re-
2. Ring the bells of heav-en! there is joy to-day, For the wan-d'rer
3. Ring the bells of heav-en! spread the feast to-day, An-gels, swell the

turn-ing from the wild; See! the Fa-ther meets him out up-on the way,
now is rec-on-ciled; Yes, a soul is res-cued from his sin-ful way,
glad tri-um-phant strain! Tell the joy-ful ti-dings, bear it far a-way!

Chorus

Wel-com-ing His wea-ry, wan-d'ring child.
And is born a-new a ran-somed child. Glo-ry! glo-ry! how the
For a pre-cious soul is born a-gain.

an-gels sing; Glo-ry! glo-ry! how the loud harps ring! 'Tis the ran-somed

ar-my, like a might-y sea, Peal-ing forth the an-them of the free.

29 Have Thine Own Way, Lord

A. A. P.

GEO. C. STEBBINS

Slowly

1. Have Thine own way, Lord! Have Thine own way!.. Thou art the
2. Have Thine own way, Lord! Have Thine own way!.. Search me and
3. Have Thine own way, Lord! Have Thine own way!.. Wound-ed and
4. Have Thine own way, Lord! Have Thine own way!.. Hold o'er my

Pot - ter; I am the clay... Mould me and make me Aft - er Thy
try me, Mas-ter, to - day!... Whit - er than snow, Lord, Wash me just
wea - ry, Help me, I pray!. Pow - er—all pow - er—Sure - ly is
be - ing Ab - so - lute sway!. Fill with Thy Spir - it Till all shall

will,... While I am wait - ing, Yield - ed and still...
now,... As in Thy pres - ence Hum - bly I bow...
Thine! Touch me and heal me, Sav - ior di - vine!..
see.... Christ on - ly, al - ways, Liv - ing in me!....

30 My Faith Looks Up to Thee

RAY PALMER

LOWELL MASON

1. My faith looks up to Thee, Thou Lamb of Cal - va - ry,
2. May Thy rich grace im - part Strength to my faint - ing heart,
3. While life's dark maze I tread, And griefs a - round me spread,

My Faith Looks Up to Thee

Sav - ior di - vine; Now hear me when I pray, Take all my
My zeal in - spire; As Thou hast died for me, O may my
Be Thou my Guide; Bid dark - ness turn to day, Wipe sor - row's

sin a - way, O let me from this day Be whol - ly Thine!
love to Thee, Pure, warm, and changeless be,—A liv - ing fire!
tears a - way, Nor let me ev - er stray From Thee a - side.

31 O Happy Day

PHILIP DODDRIDGE

E. F. RIMBAULT

1. { O hap - py day that fixed my choice On Thee, my Sav - ior and my God! }
{ Well may this glow-ing heart re - joice, And tell its rap - tures all a - broad. }
2. { O hap - py bond, that seals my vows To Him who mer - its all my love! }
{ Let cheer-ful an-thems fill His house, While to that sa - cred shrine I move. }
3. { 'Tis done: the great trans-ac-tion's done; I am my Lord's, and He is mine; }
{ He drew me, and I fol-lowed on, Charmed to confess the voice di-vine. }
4. { Now rest, my long-di - vid - ed heart; Fixed on this bliss - ful cen - tre, rest; }
{ Nor ev - er from my Lord de - part, With Him of ev - 'ry good possessed. }

FINE

Hap - py day, hap - py day, When Je - sus washed my sins a - way!

D. S.

He taught me how to watch and pray, And live re - joic - ing ev - 'ry day;

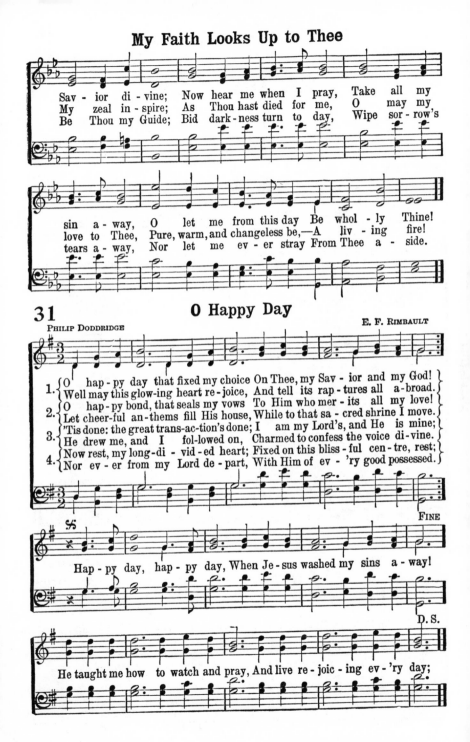

32 At the Cross

Isaac Watts   Copyright, 1916. Renewal. Mrs. Mary Hudson, owner   R. E. Hudson

1. {A - las! and did my Sav - ior bleed? And did my Sov-'reign die?
   {Would He de-vote that sa - (Omit . . . .)
2. {Was it for crimes that I have done, He groaned up-on the tree?
   {A - maz-ing pit - y! grace (Omit . . . .)

cred head For such a worm as I?
un-known! And love be - yond de-gree!

CHORUS

At the cross, at the cross, where I first saw the light, And the burden of my heart rolled away, (rolled away,) It was there by faith I re-ceived my sight, And now I am happy all the day.

33 Where He Leads Me

E. W. Blandly   J. S. Norris

1. I can hear my Sav - ior call - ing, I can hear my Sav - ior call - ing,
2. I'll go with Him thro' the gar - den, I'll go with Him thro' the gar - den,
3. I'll go with Him thro' the judg-ment, I'll go with Him thro' the judg-ment,
4. He will give me grace and glo - ry, He will give me grace and glo - ry,

REF.—*Where He leads me I will fol - low, Where He leads me I will fol - low,*

Where He Leads Me

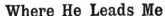

I can hear my Sav - ior call - ing, "Take thy cross and fol - low, fol - low Me."
I'll go with Him thro' the gar - den, I'll go with Him, with Him all the way.
I'll go with Him thro' the judg-ment, I'll go with Him, with Him all the way.
He will give me grace and glo - ry, And go with me, with me all the way.

Where He leads me I will fol - low, I'll go with Him, with Him all the way.

34 Something For Jesus

S. D. PHELPS

ROBERT LOWRY

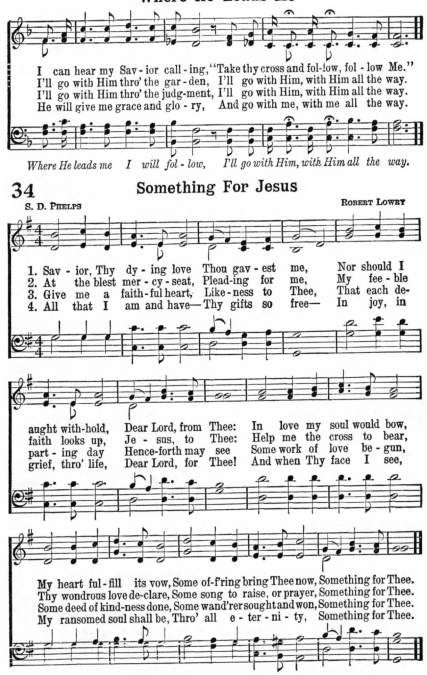

1. Sav - ior, Thy dy - ing love Thou gav - est me, Nor should I
2. At the blest mer - cy-seat, Plead-ing for me, My fee - ble
3. Give me a faith-ful heart, Like-ness to Thee, That each de-
4. All that I am and have—Thy gifts so free— In joy, in

aught with-hold, Dear Lord, from Thee: In love my soul would bow,
faith looks up, Je - sus, to Thee: Help me the cross to bear,
part - ing day Hence-forth may see Some work of love be - gun,
grief, thro' life, Dear Lord, for Thee! And when Thy face I see,

My heart ful - fill its vow, Some of-f'ring bring Thee now, Something for Thee.
Thy wondrous love de-clare, Some song to raise, or prayer, Something for Thee.
Some deed of kind-ness done, Some wand'rer sought and won, Something for Thee.
My ransomed soul shall be, Thro' all e - ter - ni - ty, Something for Thee.

35 Dwelling in Beulah Land

C. A. M.

C. Austin Miles

1. Far a-way the noise of strife up-on my ear is fall-ing, Then I know the
2. Far be-low the storm of doubt up-on the world is beat-ing, Sons of men in
3. Let the storm-y breez-es blow, their cry can-not a-larm me; I am safe-ly
4. Viewing here the works of God, I sink in con-tem-pla-tion, Hearing now His

sins of earth be-set on ev-'ry hand: Doubt and fear and things of earth in
bat-tle long the en-e-my with-stand: Safe am I with-in the cas-tle
sheltered here, pro-tect-ed by God's hand: Here the sun is al-ways shin-ing,
bless-ed voice, I see the way He planned: Dwell-ing in the Spir-it, here I

vain to me are call-ing, None of these shall move me from Beu-lah Land.
of God's word re-treat-ing, Nothing then can reach me—'tis Beu-lah Land.
here there's naught can harm me, I am safe for-ev-er in Beu-lah Land.
learn of full sal-va-tion, Glad-ly will I tar-ry in Beu-lah Land.

Chorus

I'm liv-ing on the moun-tain, un-der-neath a cloud-less sky, I'm
Praise God!

drink-ing at the foun-tain that never shall run dry; O yes! I'm feasting on the

Dwelling In Beulah Land

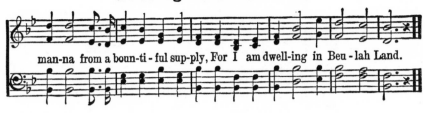

man-na from a boun-ti-ful sup-ply, For I am dwell-ing in Beu-lah Land.

36   Wonderful Words Of Life

P. P. B.

P. P. Bliss

1. Sing them o - ver a - gain to me, Won-der - ful words of Life;
2. Christ, the bless - ed One, gives to all, Won-der - ful words of Life;
3. Sweet - ly ech - o the gos - pel call, Won-der - ful words of Life;

Let me more of their beau - ty see, Won-der - ful words of Life.
Sin - ner, list to the lov - ing call, Won-der - ful words of Life.
Of - fer par - don and peace to all, Won-der - ful words of Life.

Words of life and beau - ty, Teach me faith and du - ty:
All so free - ly giv - en, Woo - ing us to heav - en:
Je - sus, on - ly Sav - ior, Sanc - ti - fy for - ev - er:

REFRAIN

Beau-ti-ful words, won-der-ful words, Won-der - ful words of Life. Life.

37 Can the World See Jesus in You?

Mrs. C. H. M.

Mrs. C. H. Morris

1. Do we live so close to the Lord to-day, Pass-ing to and fro on life's
2. Do we love, with love to His own a - kin, All His creatures lost in the
3. As an o - pen book they our lives will read, To our words and acts giv-ing

bus - y way, That the world in us can a like - ness see To the
mire of sin? Will we reach a hand, what-so - e'er it cost, To re-
dai - ly heed; Will they be at - tract - ed, or turn a - way From the

CHORUS

Man of Cal - va - ry?.... Can the world see Je - sus in me? Can the
claim a sin - ner lost?... Can the world see Je - sus in me? Can the
Christ we love to - day?...
Man of Cal - va - ry? Can the world see Je - sus in me?

world see Je - sus in you? Does your love to Him ring true,
Can the world see........ Je - sus in you?

And your life and serv - ice, too? Can the world see Je - sus in you?
me — in you?

38 There is Glory in My Soul

GRACE WEISER DAVIS

CHAS. H. GABRIEL

1. Since I lost my sins and I found my Sav-ior, There is glo-ry in my soul!
2. Since He cleansed my heart, gave me sight for blindness, There is glo-ry in my soul!
3. Since with God I've walked, having sweet communion, There is glo-ry in my soul!
4. Since I entered Canaan on my way to heav-en, There is glo-ry in my soul!

Since by faith I sought and obtained God's fa-vor, There is glo-ry in my soul!
Since He touched and healed me in loving kindness, There is glo-ry in my soul!
Brighter grows each day in this heav'nly un-ion, There is glo-ry in my soul!
Since the day my life to the Lord was giv-en, There is glo-ry in my soul!

CHORUS

There is glo-ry, glo-ry, there is glo-ry in my soul! Ev-'ry

day brighter grows, And I con-quer all my foes; There is glo-ry, glo-ry,

there is glo-ry in my soul! There is glo-ry in my soul!
glo-ry in my soul!

39 Count Your Blessings

Rev. Johnson Oatman, Jr.

E. O. Excell

1. When up-on life's bil-lows you are tem-pest-tossed, When you are dis-
2. Are you ev-er bur-dened with a load of care? Does the cross seem
3. When you look at oth-ers with their lands and gold, Think that Christ has
4. So, a-mid the con-flict, whether great or small, Do not be dis-

cour-aged, think-ing all is lost, Count your man-y bless-ings, name them
heav-y you are called to bear? Count your man-y bless-ings, ev-'ry
prom-ised you His wealth un-told; Count your man-y bless-ings, mon-ey
cour-aged, God is o-ver all; Count your man-y bless-ings, an-gels

one by one, And it will sur-prise you what the Lord hath done.
doubt will fly, And you will be sing-ing as the days go by.
can-not buy Your re-ward in Heav-en, nor your home on high.
will at-tend, Help and com-fort give you to your jour-ney's end.

Chorus.

Count your bless-ings, Name them one by one; Count your
Count your man-y bless-ings, Name them one by one; Count your man-y

bless-ings, See what God hath done; Count your bless-ings,
bless-ings, See what God hath done; Count your man-y bless-ings,

Count Your Blessings

Name them one by one; Count your man-y blessings, See what God hath done.

40   'Tis So Sweet to Trust in Jesus

LOUISA M. R. STEAD

WM. J. KIRKPATRICK

1. 'Tis so sweet to trust in Je-sus, Just to take Him at His Word;
2. O how sweet to trust in Je-sus, Just to trust His cleans-ing blood;
3. Yes,'tis sweet to trust in Je-sus, Just from sin and self to cease;
4. I'm so glad I learned to trust Thee, Pre-cious Je-sus, Sav-ior, Friend;

Just to rest up-on His prom-ise; Just to know,"Thus saith the Lord."
Just in sim-ple faith to plunge me 'Neath the heal-ing, cleans-ing flood!
Just from Je-sus sim-ply tak-ing Life and rest, and joy and peace.
And I know that Thou art with me, Wilt be with me to the end.

CHORUS

Je-sus, Je-sus, how I trust Him! How I've proved Him o'er and o'er!

Je-sus, Je-sus, pre-cious Je-sus! O for grace to trust Him more!

Copyright, 1882 and 1910, by Wm. J. Kirkpatrick. Hope Publishing Co., owner

41   In My Heart There Rings a Melody

E. M. R.

ELTON M. ROTH

1. I have a song that Je-sus gave me, It was sent from
2. I love the Christ who died on Cal-v'ry, For He washed my
3. 'Twill be my end-less theme in glo-ry, With the an-gels

heav'n a-bove; There nev-er was a sweet-er mel-o-dy, 'Tis a
sins a-way; He put with-in my heart a mel-o-dy, And I
I will sing; 'Twill be a song with glo-rious har-mo-ny, When the

CHORUS

mel-o-dy of love.
know it's there to stay.   In my heart there rings a mel-o-dy, There
courts of heav-en ring.

rings a mel-o-dy with heav-en's har-mo-ny; In my heart there

rings a mel-o-dy; There rings a mel-o-dy of love.

43   There Shall Be Showers of Blessing

EL NATHAN   JAMES McGRANAHAN

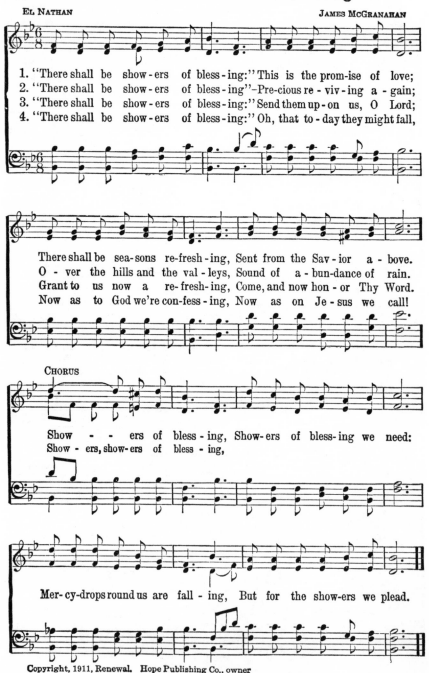

1. "There shall be show-ers of bless-ing:" This is the prom-ise of love;
2. "There shall be show-ers of bless-ing"–Pre-cious re - viv-ing a - gain;
3. "There shall be show-ers of bless-ing:" Send them up-on us, O Lord;
4. "There shall be show-ers of bless-ing:" Oh, that to - day they might fall,

There shall be sea-sons re-fresh-ing, Sent from the Sav-ior a - bove.
O - ver the hills and the val - leys, Sound of a - bun-dance of rain.
Grant to us now a re-fresh-ing, Come, and now hon - or Thy Word.
Now as to God we're con-fess-ing, Now as on Je - sus we call!

CHORUS

Show - - ers of bless-ing, Show-ers of bless-ing we need:
Show - ers, show-ers of bless - ing,

Mer- cy-drops round us are fall - ing, But for the show-ers we plead.

44 Oh! Say, But I'm Glad

Dedicated to Bishop Arthur J. Moore

Rev. Jas. P. Sullivan

Mildred Ellen Sullivan

mf

1. There is a song in my heart to-day, Something I nev-er had; ..
2. Won-der-ful, mar-vel-ous love He brings, In - to a heart that's sad; ..
3. We have a fel-low-ship rich and sweet, Tongue can nev-er re - late; ..
4. Won't you come to Him with all your care, Wea-ry and worn and sad? ..

Je - sus has tak-en my sins a - way, Oh! say, but I'm glad.
Thro' darkest tun-nels the soul just sings, Oh! say, but I'm glad.
Abid-ing in Him is a re - al treat, Oh! say, but it's great.
You too, will sing as His love you share, Oh! say, but I'm glad.

CHORUS

Oh! say, but I'm glad, I'm glad, Oh! say, but I'm glad; *(Inst.)*

f

Je-sus has come and my cup's o - ver run, Oh! say, but I'm glad.

45 Jesus is All the World to Me

W. L. T.

WILL L. THOMPSON

1. Je - sus is all the world to me, My life, my joy, my all;
2. Je - sus is all the world to me, My Friend in tri - als sore;
3. Je - sus is all the world to me, And true to Him I'll be;
4. Je - sus is all the world to me, I want no bet - ter friend;

He is my strength from day to day, With - out Him I would fall.
I go to Him for bless-ings, and He gives them o'er and o'er.
Oh, how could I this Friend de - ny, When He's so true to me?
I trust Him now, I'll trust Him when Life's fleet - ing days shall end.

When I am sad, to Him I go, No oth - er one can
He sends the sun - shine and the rain, He sends the har - vest's
Fol - low - ing Him I know I'm right, He watch - es o'er me
Beau - ti - ful life with such a Friend; Beau - ti - ful life that

cheer me so; When I am sad He makes me glad, He's my Friend.
gold - en grain; Sun-shine and rain, har - vest of grain, He's my Friend.
day and night; Fol - low - ing Him, by day and night, He's my Friend.
has no end; E - ter - nal life, e - ter - nal joy, He's my Friend.

46 *Tell It Again

Mrs. M. B. C. SLADE

R. M. McINTOSH

1. In - to a tent where a gip - sy boy lay, Dy - ing a - lone, at the
2. "Did He so love me, a poor lit - tle boy? Send un - to me the good
3. Bending, we caught the last words of his breath, Just as he en - tered the
4. Smil - ing, he said, as his last sigh was spent, "I am so glad that for

close of the day, News of sal - va - tion we car - ried; said he:
ti - dings of joy? Need I not per - ish?—my hand will He hold?
val - ley of death: "God sent His Son!—who - so - ev - er!" said he;
me He was sent!" Whis - pered, while low sank the sun in the west:

D. S.—*Till none can say of the chil - dren of men,*

FINE. CHORUS

"No - bod - y ev - er has told it to me!"
No - bod - y ev - er the sto - ry has told!" Tell it a - gain!
"Then I am sure that He sent Him for me!"
"Lord, I be - lieve! tell it now to the rest!"

"No - bod - y ev - er has told me be - fore!"

D. S.

tell it a - gain! Sal - va - tion's sto - ry re - peat o'er and o'er,

*A home missionary visited a dying boy in a gipsy tent; bending over him, he said: "God so loved the world, that He gave His only Son, that whosoever believeth in Him should not perish, but have everlasting life." The dying boy heard and whispered: "Nobody ever told me."

47 Praise Him! Praise Him!

FANNY J. CROSBY

CHESTER G. ALLEN

1. Praise Him! praise Him! Je-sus, our bless-ed Re-deem-er! Sing, O Earth, His won-der-ful love pro-claim! Hail Him! hail Him! highest archangels in glo-ry; Strength and hon-or give to His ho-ly name! Like a shep-herd, Je-sus will guard His children, In His arms He carries them all day long:
2. Praise Him! praise Him! Je-sus, our bless-ed Re-deem-er! For our sins He suffered, and bled, and died; He our Rock, our hope of e-ter-nal sal-va-tion, Hail Him! hail Him! Je-sus the Cru-ci-fied. Sound His praises! Je-sus who bore our sorrows, Love unbounded, wonderful, deep and strong: Praise Him! praise Him!
3. Praise Him! praise Him! Je-sus, our bless-ed Re-deem-er! Heav'nly por-tals loud with ho-san-nas ring! Je-sus, Sav-ior, reigneth for-ev-er and ev-er; Crown Him! crown Him! Prophet, and Priest, and King! Christ is com-ing! o-ver the world vic-to-rious, Pow'r and glo-ry un-to the Lord be-long:

REFRAIN

tell of His ex-cel-lent greatness; Praise Him! praise Him! ev-er in joy-ful song!

48 Since Jesus Came Into My Heart

R. H. McDaniel

CHAS. H. GABRIEL

1. What a won-der-ful change in my life has been wrought Since Je-sus came
2. I have ceased from my wand'ring and go-ing a-stray, Since Je-sus came
3. I'm pos-sessed of a hope that is stead-fast and sure, Since Je-sus came
4. There's a light in the val-ley of death now for me, Since Je-sus came
5. I shall go there to dwell in that Cit-y, I know, Since Je-sus came

in-to my heart! I have light in my soul for which long I had sought,
in-to my heart! And my sins, which were man-y, are all washed a-way,
in-to my heart! And no dark clouds of doubt now my path-way ob-scure,
in-to my heart! And the gates of the Cit-y be-yond I can see,
in-to my heart! And I'm hap-py, so hap-py, as on-ward I go,

CHORUS

Since Je-sus came in-to my heart! Since Je-sus came in-to my
Since Je-sus came in, came

heart, Since Je-sus came in-to my heart, Floods of joy o'er my
in-to my heart, Since Je-sus came in, came in-to my heart,

soul like the sea bil-lows roll, Since Je-sus came in-to my heart.

49 Standing On the Promises

R. K. C.

R. KELSO CARTER

1. Stand-ing on the prom-is-es of Christ my King, Thro' e-ter-nal a-ges
2. Stand-ing on the prom-is-es that can-not fail, When the howling storms of
3. Stand-ing on the prom-is-es of Christ the Lord, Bound to Him e-ter-nal-
4. Stand-ing on the prom-is-es I can-not fall, Lis-t'ning ev-'ry mo-ment

let His prais-es ring; Glo-ry in the high-est, I will shout and sing,
doubt and fear as-sail, By the liv-ing word of God I shall pre-vail,
ly by love's strong cord, O-ver-com-ing dai-ly with the Spir-it's sword,
to the Spir-it's call, Rest-ing in my Sav-ior, as my all in all,

CHORUS

Stand-ing on the prom-is-es of God. Stand - - ing, stand - - ing,
Standing on the promises, standing on the promises,

Stand-ing on the prom-is-es of God my Sav-ior; Stand - - ing,
Stand-ing on the prom-is-es,

stand - - ing, I'm stand-ing on the prom-is-es of God.
stand-ing on the prom-is-es,

50 Some Bright Morning

Copyright, 1926, by Homer A. Rodeheaver
International copyright secured

CHARLOTTE G. HOMER

CHAS. H. GABRIEL

1. Be not a-wea-ry, for la-bor will cease Some glad morn-ing;
2. Wea-ri-some bur-dens will all be laid down, Some glad morn-ing;
3. La-bor well done shall re-ceive its re-ward, Some glad morn-ing;
4. O what a time of re-joic-ing will come, Some glad morn-ing;
5. There with the loved ones who've gone on be-fore, Some glad morn-ing;

Tur-moil will change in-to in-fi-nite peace, Some bright morn-ing.
Then shall our cross be exchanged for a crown, Some bright morn-ing.
Thou who art faith-ful shall be with the Lord, Some bright morn-ing.
When all the ransomed are gathered at home, Some bright morn-ing.
We shall sing praise to the Lamb ev-er-more, Some bright morn-ing.

CHORUS

Some bright morning, Some glad morn-ing, When the sun is shin-ing in th' e-ter-nal sky; .... Some bright morn-ing, Some glad morn-ing .. *cres.* We shall see the Lord of Har-vest, By and by.

51 Wonderful Jesus

ANNIE B. RUSSELL
Copyright, 1921, by Ernest O. Sellers
ERNEST O. SELLERS

1. There is nev-er a day so drear-y, There is nev-er a
2. There is nev-er a cross so heav-y, There is nev-er a
3. There is nev-er a care or bur-den, There is nev-er a
4. There is nev-er a guilt-y sin-ner, There is nev-er a

night so long, (so long,) But the soul that is trusting Je-sus Will
weight of woe, (of woe,) But that Je-sus will help to car-ry Be-
grief or loss, (or loss,) But that Je-sus in love will light-en When
wan-d'ring one, (not one,) But that God can in mer-cy par-don Thro'

somewhere find a song. (a song.)
cause He lov-eth so. (loves so.) Won-der-ful, won-der-ful Je-sus,
car-ried to the cross. (the cross.)
Je-sus Christ, His Son. (His Son.)

CHORUS

In the heart He im-plant-eth a song; .... A song of de-liv-'rance, of
He planteth a song;

cour-age, of strength, In the heart He im-plant-eth a song. (a song.)

52   Songs of Praises

Rev. William Williams

Wm. Owen

1. Guide me, O Thou great Je - ho - vah, Pil - grim thro' this bar - ren land;
2. O - pen now the crys - tal foun - tain, Whence the heal - ing wa - ters flow;
3. When I tread the verge of Jor - dan, Bid my anx - ious fears sub - side;

I am weak, but Thou art might - y; Hold me with Thy pow'r-ful hand:
Let the fi - er - y, cloud - y pil - lar Lead me all my jour-ney through:
Bear me thro' the swell-ing cur - rent; Land me safe on Ca-naan's side:

Bread of heav - en, Bread of heav - en, Bread of heav - en,
Strong De-liv - 'rer, Strong De-liv - 'rer, Strong De-liv - 'rer,
Songs of prais - es, Songs of prais - es, Songs of prais - es
1. Bread of heav - en, Bread of heav - en, Bread of heav - en,

Feed me till I want no more, Feed me till I want no more.
Be Thou still my strength and shield, Be Thou still my strength and shield.
I will ev - er give to Thee, I will ev - er give to Thee.

53 Just As I Am

CHARLOTTE ELLIOTT

WILLIAM B. BRADBURY

1. Just as I am, with-out one plea, But that Thy blood was shed for me,
2. Just as I am, and waiting not To rid my soul of one dark blot,
3. Just as I am, tho' tossed a-bout With many a con-flict, many a doubt,
4. Just as I am, poor, wretched, blind; Sight, rich-es, heal-ing of the mind,
5. Just as I am—Thou wilt re-ceive, Wilt welcome, pardon, cleanse, relieve;

And that Thou bidd'st me come to Thee, O Lamb of God, I come! I come!
To Thee whose blood can cleanse each spot, O Lamb of God, I come! I come!
Fight-ings and fears with-in, with-out, O Lamb of God, I come! I come!
Yea, all I need in Thee to find, O Lamb of God, I come! I come!
Be-cause Thy promise I be-lieve, O Lamb of God, I come! I come!

54 Only Trust Him

J. H. S.

J. H. STOCKTON

1. Come, ev - 'ry soul by sin oppressed, There's mer-cy with the Lord,
2. For Je - sus shed His pre-cious blood, Rich bless-ings to be - stow;
3. Yes, Je - sus is the Truth, the Way, That leads you in - to rest:
4. Come, then, and join this ho - ly band, And on to glo - ry go,

And He will sure - ly give you rest By trust-ing in His word.
Plunge now in - to the crim - son flood That wash - es white as snow.
Be - lieve in Him with - out de - lay, And you are ful - ly blest.
To dwell in that ce - les - tial land, Where joys im - mor - tal flow.

Only Trust Him

CHORUS

{ On - ly trust Him, on - ly trust Him, On - ly trust Him now; }
{ He will save you, He will save you, He will (*Omit* . . . .) } save you now.

55 Leaning On the Everlasting Arms

E. A. HOFFMAN   A. J. SHOWALTER

1. What a fel-low-ship, what a joy di-vine, Leaning on the ev-er-last-ing arms;
2. Oh, how sweet to walk in this pilgrim way, Leaning on the ev-er-last-ing arms;
3. What have I to dread, what have I to fear, Leaning on the ev-er-last-ing arms?

What a bless-ed-ness, what a peace is mine, Leaning on the ev-er-last-ing arms.
Oh, how bright the path grows from day to day, Leaning on the ev-er-last-ing arms.
I have bless-ed peace with my Lord so near, Leaning on the ev-er-last-ing arms.

REFRAIN

Lean - ing, lean - ing, Safe and se-cure from all a-larms;
Lean-ing on Je - sus, lean-ing on Je - sus,

Lean - ing, lean - ing, Lean-ing on the ev-er-last-ing arms.
Lean-ing on Je - sus, lean-ing on Je - sus,

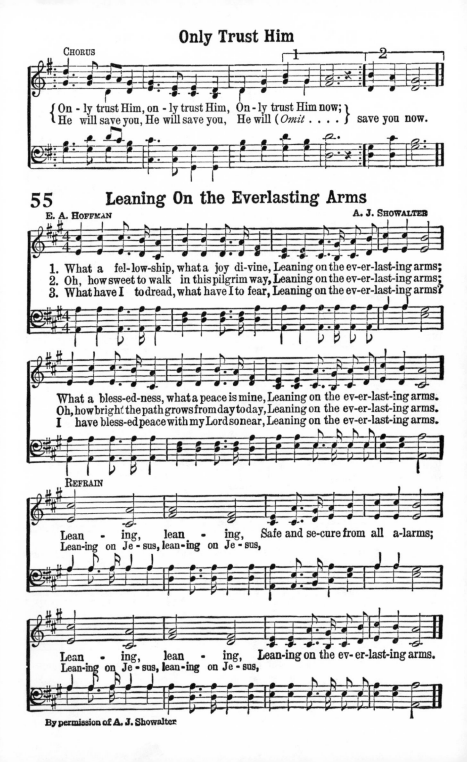

By permission of A. J. Showalter

56 He's a Wonderful Savior to Me

VIRGIL P. BROCK

BLANCHE KERR BROCK

1. I was lost in sin but Je-sus res-cued me, He's a won-der-ful Sav-ior to me;
2. He's a Friend so true, so pa-tient and so kind, He's a won-der-ful Sav-ior to me;
3. He is al-ways near to com-fort and to cheer, He's a won-der-ful Sav-ior to me;
4. Dearer grows the love of Je-sus day by day, He's a won-der-ful Sav-ior to me;

So won-der-ful!

I was bound by fear but Je-sus set me free, He's a
Ev-'ry-thing I need in Him I al-ways find, He's a
He for-gives my sins, He dries my ev-'ry tear, He's a
Sweeter is His grace while pressing on my way, He's a

CHORUS

won-der-ful Sav-ior to me............ For He's a won-der-ful

So won-der-ful!

Sav-ior to me, He's a won-der-ful Sav-ior to me; I was

won-der-ful! won-der-ful!

lost in sin, but Je-sus took me in, He's a won-der-ful Sav-ior to me.

57 My Mother's Bible

Evangelist M. B. WILLIAMS

CHARLIE D. TILLMAN

DUET

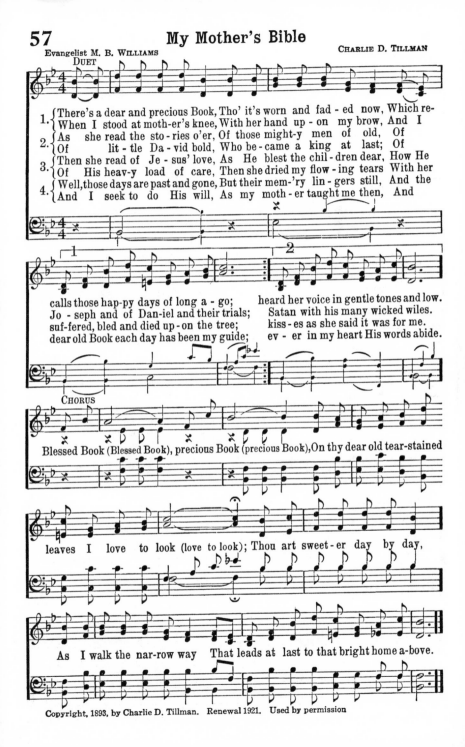

1. There's a dear and precious Book, Tho' it's worn and fad-ed now, Which re-
When I stood at moth-er's knee, With her hand up-on my brow, And I
2. As she read the sto-ries o'er, Of those might-y men of old, Of
Of lit-tle Da-vid bold, Who be-came a king at last; Of
3. Then she read of Je-sus' love, As He blest the chil-dren dear, How He
Of His heav-y load of care, Then she dried my flow-ing tears With her
4. Well, those days are past and gone, But their mem-'ry lin-gers still, And the
And I seek to do His will, As my moth-er taught me then, And

calls those hap-py days of long a-go; heard her voice in gentle tones and low.
Jo-seph and of Dan-iel and their trials; Satan with his many wicked wiles.
suf-fered, bled and died up-on the tree; kiss-es as she said it was for me.
dear old Book each day has been my guide; ev-er in my heart His words abide.

CHORUS

Blessed Book (Blessed Book), precious Book (precious Book), On thy dear old tear-stained

leaves I love to look (love to look); Thou art sweet-er day by day,

As I walk the nar-row way That leads at last to that bright home a-bove.

Copyright, 1893, by Charlie D. Tillman. Renewal 1921. Used by permission

58 He Ransomed Me

JULIA H. JOHNSTON

J. W. HENDERSON

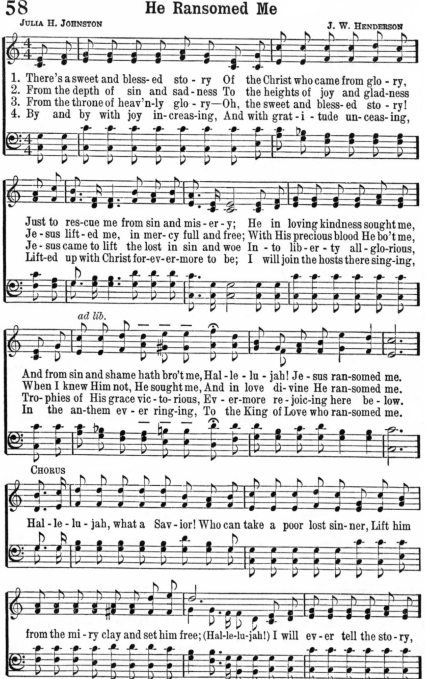

1. There's a sweet and bless-ed sto-ry Of the Christ who came from glo-ry,
2. From the depth of sin and sad-ness To the heights of joy and glad-ness
3. From the throne of heav'n-ly glo-ry—Oh, the sweet and bless-ed sto-ry!
4. By and by with joy in-creas-ing, And with grat-i-tude un-ceas-ing,

Just to res-cue me from sin and mis-er-y; He in loving kindness sought me,
Je-sus lift-ed me, in mer-cy full and free; With His precious blood He bo't me,
Je-sus came to lift the lost in sin and woe In-to lib-er-ty all-glo-rious,
Lift-ed up with Christ for-ev-er-more to be; I will join the hosts there sing-ing,

ad lib.

And from sin and shame hath bro't me, Hal-le-lu-jah! Je-sus ran-somed me.
When I knew Him not, He sought me, And in love di-vine He ran-somed me.
Tro-phies of His grace vic-to-rious, Ev-er-more re-joic-ing here be-low.
In the an-them ev-er ring-ing, To the King of Love who ran-somed me.

CHORUS

Hal-le-lu-jah, what a Sav-ior! Who can take a poor lost sin-ner, Lift him

from the mi-ry clay and set him free; (Hal-le-lu-jah!) I will ev-er tell the sto-ry,

He Ransomed Me

Shout-ing glo - ry, glo - ry, glo - ry, Hal - le - lu - jah! Je - sus ran - somed me.

59 Nothing But the Blood

R. L.

ROBERT LOWRY

1. What can wash a - way my sin? Noth-ing but the blood of Je - sus;
2. For my par - don this I see— Noth-ing but the blood of Je - sus;
3. Noth - ing can for sin a - tone— Noth-ing but the blood of Je - sus;
4. This is all my hope and peace—Noth-ing but the blood of Je - sus;

What can make me whole a - gain? Noth-ing but the blood of Je - sus.
For my cleans-ing, this my plea—Noth-ing but the blood of Je - sus.
Naught of good that I have done—Noth-ing but the blood of Je - sus.
This is all my right-eous-ness—Noth-ing but the blood of Je - sus.

REFRAIN

Oh! pre - cious is the flow That makes me white as snow;

No oth - er fount I know, Noth-ing but the blood of Je - sus.

60 Help Somebody To-day

Mrs. Frank A. Breck

Chas. H. Gabriel

1. Look all a-round you, find some one in need, Help some-bod-y to - day!
2. Man - y are wait-ing a kind, lov-ing word, Help some-bod-y to - day!
3. Man - y have bur-dens too heav - y to bear, Help some-bod-y to - day!
4. Some are dis-cour-aged and wear-y in heart, Help some-bod-y to - day!

Tho' it be lit - tle—a neigh-bor - ly deed—Help some-bod - y to - day!
Thou hast a mes-sage, O let it be heard, Help some-bod - y to - day!
Grief is the por - tion of some ev - 'ry-where, Help some-bod - y to - day!
Some one the jour-ney to Heaven should start, Help some-bod - y to - day!

CHORUS.

Help some-bod - y to - day, . . Some-bod - y a - long life's way; . . Let
to-day,   home-ward way;

sorrow be ended, The friendless befriended, Oh, help somebody to-day! A - MEN.

61 Trust and Obey

J. H. SAMMIS

D. B. TOWNER

1. When we walk with the Lord In the Light of His Word What a glo-ry He
2. Not a shad-ow can rise, Not a cloud in the skies, But His smile quickly
3. Not a bur-den we bear, Not a sor-row we share, But our toil He doth
4. But we nev-er can prove The de-lights of His love Un-til all on the
5. Then in fel-low-ship sweet We will sit at His feet, Or we'll walk by His

sheds on our way! While we do His good-will, He a-bides with us still,
drives it a-way; Not a doubt or a fear, Not a sigh nor a tear,
rich-ly re-pay; Not a grief nor a loss, Not a frown or a cross,
al-tar we lay; For the fa-vor He shows, And the joy He be-stows,
side in the way; What He says we will do, Where He sends we will go,—

CHORUS.

And with all who will trust and o-bey.
Can a-bide while we trust and o-bey.
But is blest if we trust and o-bey. Trust and o-bey, for there's no oth-er
Are for them who will trust and o-bey.
Nev-er fear, on-ly trust and o-bey.

way To be hap-py in Je-sus, But to trust and o-bey. A-MEN.

62 Pass Me Not

FANNY J. CROSBY

W. H. DOANE

1. Pass me not, O gen-tle Sav-ior, Hear my hum-ble cry; While on oth-ers
2. Let me at a throne of mer-cy Find a sweet re-lief; Kneel-ing there in
3. Trust-ing on-ly in Thy mer-it, Would I seek Thy face; Heal my wounded,
4. Thou the Spring of all my com-fort, More than life to me, Whom have I on

CHORUS

Thou art call-ing, Do not pass me by.
deep con-tri-tion, Help my un-be-lief. Sav-ior, Sav-ior, Hear my humble
bro-ken spir-it, Save me by Thy grace.
earth beside Thee? Whom in Heav'n but Thee?

cry; While on oth-ers Thou art call-ing, Do not pass me by.

63 Let the Lower Lights Be Burning

P. P. B.

P. P. BLISS

1. Bright-ly beams our Fa-ther's mer-cy From His light-house ev-er-more,
2. Dark the night of sin has set-tled, Loud the an-gry bil-lows roar;
3. Trim your fee-ble lamp, my broth-er: Some poor sail-or tem-pest-tossed,

FINE

But to us He gives the keep-ing Of the lights a-long the shore.
Ea-ger eyes are watching, long-ing, For the lights a-long the shore.
Try-ing now to make the har-bor, In the dark-ness may be lost.

D.S.—*Some poor faint-ing, struggling sea-man You may res-cue, you may save.*

Let the Lower Lights Be Burning

CHORUS

Let the low-er lights be burn-ing! Send a gleam a-cross the wave!

64   Shall We Gather At the River?

R. L.

ROBERT LOWRY

1. Shall we gath-er at the riv-er, Where bright an-gel feet have trod;
2. On the bos-om of the riv-er, Where the Sav-ior-King we own,
3. Ere we reach the shin-ing riv-er, Lay we ev-'ry bur-den down;
4. Soon we'll reach the shining riv-er, Soon our pil-grim-age will cease;

With its crys-tal tide for-ev-er Flow-ing by the throne of God?
We shall meet, and sor-row nev-er, 'Neath the glo-ry of the throne.
Grace our spir-its will de-liv-er, And pro-vide a robe and crown.
Soon our hap-py hearts will qui-ver With the mel-o-dy of peace.

CHORUS

Yes, we'll gather at the riv-er, The beau-ti-ful, the beau-ti-ful riv-er,

Gath-er with the saints at the riv-er That flows by the throne of God.

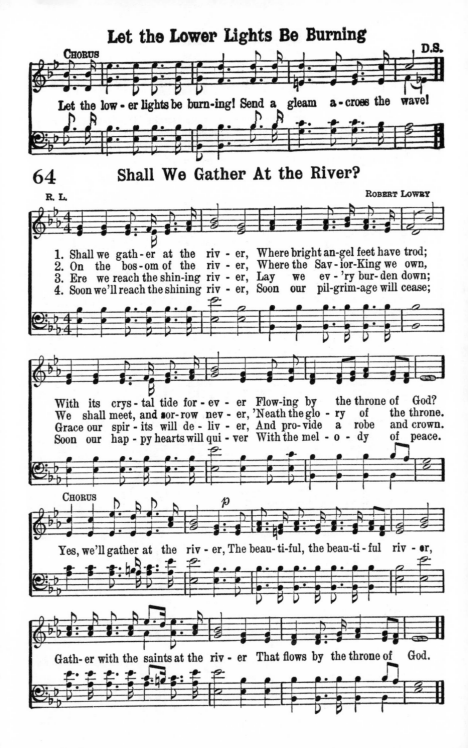

65 Loyalty to Christ

Dr. E. T. Cassel

Flora H. Cassel

1. From o-ver hill and plain There comes the signal strain, 'Tis loy-al-ty, loy-al-ty,
2. O hear, ye brave, the sound That moves the earth around, 'Tis loy-al-ty, loy-al-ty,
3. Come, join our loy-al throng, We'll rout the giant wrong, 'Tis loy-al-ty, loy-al-ty,
4. The strength of youth we lay At Je-sus' feet to-day, 'Tis loy-al-ty, loy-al-ty,

loy - al - ty to Christ; Its mu-sic rolls a-long, The hills take up the song,
loy - al - ty to Christ; A - rise to dare and do, Ring out the watch-word true,
loy - al - ty to Christ; Where Satan's banners float We'll send the bu-gle note,
loy - al - ty to Christ; His gos-pel we'll pro-claim Thro'-out the world's domain,

CHORUS.

Of loy-al-ty, loy-al-ty, Yes, loy-al-ty to Christ. "On to vic-to-ry! On to

vic-to-ry!" Cries our great Commander; "On!" . . . We'll move at His command,
great Commander; "On!"

We'll soon possess the land, Thro' loyalty, loyalty, Yes, loy-al-ty to Christ. A-MEN.

66 In The Garden

C. A. M.

(This song is based upon the meeting of Jesus and Mary on the Resurrection Morning as recorded in St. John xx: 11-18)

C. Austin Miles

1. I come to the gar-den a-lone, While the dew is still on the ros-es, And the voice I hear, Fall-ing on my ear, The Son of God dis-clos-es.

2. He speaks, and the sound of His voice Is so sweet the birds hush their sing-ing, And the mel-o-dy That He gave to me, With-in my heart is ring-ing.

3. I'd stay in the gar-den with Him Tho' the night a-round me be fall-ing, But He bids me go; Thro' the voice of woe His voice to me is call-ing.

Chorus

And He walks with me, and He talks with me, And He tells me I am His own; And the joy we share as we tar-ry there, None oth-er has ev-er known.

67 Let Him In

J. B. ATCHINSON

E. O. EXCELL

1. There's a Stran-ger at the door, Let Him in;
2. O - pen now to Him your heart, Let Him in;
3. Hear you now His lov - ing voice? Let Him in;
4. Now ad - mit the heav'n-ly Guest, Let Him in;

Let the Sav-ior in, Let the Sav-ior in;

He has been there oft be - fore, Let Him in;
If you wait He will de - part, Let Him in;
Now, oh, now make Him your choice, Let Him in;
He will make for you a feast, Let Him in;

Let the Sav-ior in, Let the Sav-ior in;

Let Him in, ere He is gone, Let Him in, the Ho - ly One, Je - sus
Let Him in, He is your Friend, He your soul will sure de - fend, He will
He is stand-ing at your door, Joy to you He will re - store, And His
He will speak your sins for-giv'n, And when earth ties all are riv'n, He will

Christ, the Fa-ther's Son, Let Him in.
keep you to the end, Let Him in.
name you will a - dore, Let Him in.
take you home to Heav'n, Let Him in.

Let the Sav-ior in, Let the Sav-ior in.

68 Jesus, I Come

W. T. SLEEPER

GEO. C. STEBBINS

1. Out of my bond-age, sor-row and night, Je-sus, I come, Je-sus, I come;
2. Out of my shame-ful fail-ure and loss, Je-sus, I come, Je-sus, I come;
3. Out of un-rest and ar-ro-gant pride, Je-sus, I come, Je-sus, I come;
4. Out of the fear and dread of the tomb, Je-sus, I come, Je-sus, I come;

In-to Thy free-dom, glad-ness and light, Je-sus, I come to Thee;
In-to the glo-rious gain of Thy cross, Je-sus, I come to Thee;
In-to Thy bless-ed will to a-bide, Je-sus, I come to Thee;
In-to the joy and light of Thy home, Je-sus, I come to Thee;

Out of my sick-ness in-to Thy health, Out of my want and in-to Thy wealth,
Out of earth's sorrows in-to Thy balm, Out of life's storms and in-to Thy calm,
Out of my-self to dwell in Thy love, Out of de-spair in-to rap-tures a-bove,
Out of the depths of ru-in un-told, In-to the peace of Thy sheltering fold,

Out of my sin and in-to Thy-self, Je-sus, I come to Thee.
Out of dis-tress to ju-bi-lant psalm, Je-sus, I come to Thee.
Up-ward for aye on wings like a dove, Je-sus, I come to Thee.
Ev-er Thy glo-rious face to be-hold, Je-sus, I come to Thee.

69 I Am Coming Home

A. H. ACKLEY   B. D. ACKLEY

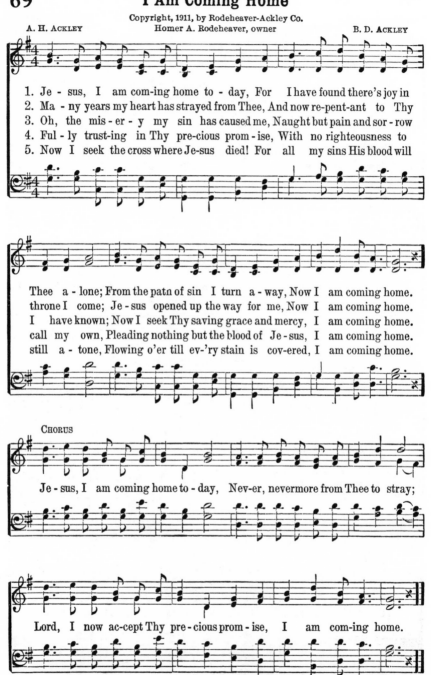

1. Je - sus, I am com-ing home to - day, For I have found there's joy in
2. Ma - ny years my heart has strayed from Thee, And now re-pent-ant to Thy
3. Oh, the mis - er - y my sin has caused me, Naught but pain and sor - row
4. Ful - ly trust-ing in Thy pre-cious prom - ise, With no righteousness to
5. Now I seek the cross where Je-sus died! For all my sins His blood will

Thee a - lone; From the path of sin I turn a - way, Now I am coming home.
throne I come; Je - sus opened up the way for me, Now I am coming home.
I have known; Now I seek Thy saving grace and mercy, I am coming home.
call my own, Pleading nothing but the blood of Je - sus, I am coming home.
still a - tone, Flowing o'er till ev-'ry stain is cov-ered, I am coming home.

CHORUS

Je - sus, I am coming home to - day, Nev-er, nevermore from Thee to stray;

Lord, I now ac-cept Thy pre - cious prom - ise, I am com-ing home.

70 The Haven of Rest

H. L. GILMOUR

GEO. D. MOORE

1. My soul in sad ex - ile was out on life's sea, So
2. I yield - ed my - self to His ten - der em - brace, And
3. The song of my soul, since the Lord made me whole, Has
4. How pre - cious the thought that we all may re - cline, Like
5. O come to the Sav - ior, He pa - tient - ly waits To

bur-dened with sin and dis - trest, Till I heard a sweet voice say-ing,
faith tak - ing hold of the Word, My fet - ters fell off, and I
been the old sto - ry so blest, Of Je - sus, who'll save who-so-
John the be - lov - ed and blest, On Je - sus' strong arm, where no
save by His pow - er di - vine; Come, an - chor your soul in the

D. S.—*The tem - pest may sweep o'er the*

Fine.

"Make me your choice;" And I en-tered the "Ha - ven of Rest!"
an - chored my soul; The "Ha - ven of Rest" is my Lord.
ev - er will have A home in the "Ha - ven of Rest!"
tem - pest can harm,— Se - cure in the "Ha - ven of Rest!"
"Ha - ven of Rest," And say, "My Be - lov - ed is mine."

wild, storm-y deep, In Je - sus I'm safe ev - er - more.

CHORUS

D. S.

I've anchored my soul in the "Ha-ven of Rest," I'll sail the wide seas no more;

71 The Unclouded Day

J. K. A.

Rev. J. K. ALWOOD

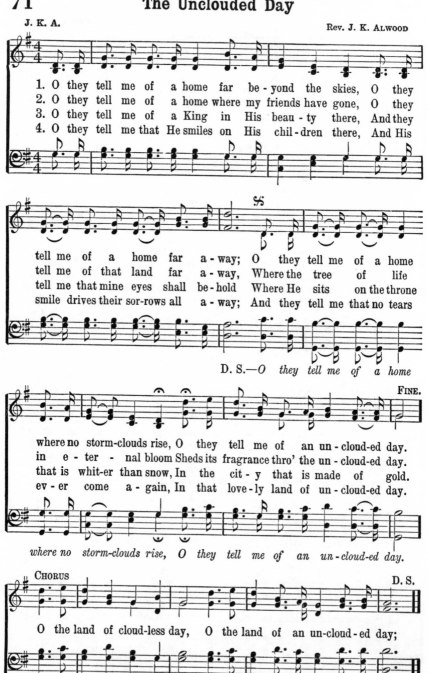

1. O they tell me of a home far be-yond the skies, O they
2. O they tell me of a home where my friends have gone, O they
3. O they tell me of a King in His beau-ty there, And they
4. O they tell me that He smiles on His chil-dren there, And His

tell me of a home far a-way; O they tell me of a home
tell me of that land far a-way, Where the tree of life
tell me that mine eyes shall be-hold Where He sits on the throne
smile drives their sor-rows all a-way; And they tell me that no tears

D. S.—*O they tell me of a home*

where no storm-clouds rise, O they tell me of an un-cloud-ed day.
in e-ter-nal bloom Sheds its fragrance thro' the un-cloud-ed day.
that is whit-er than snow, In the cit-y that is made of gold.
ev-er come a-gain, In that love-ly land of un-cloud-ed day.

where no storm-clouds rise, O they tell me of an un-cloud-ed day.

CHORUS

D. S.

O the land of cloud-less day, O the land of an un-cloud-ed day;

72   I Am Praying For You

S. O'Maley Cluff

Ira D. Sankey

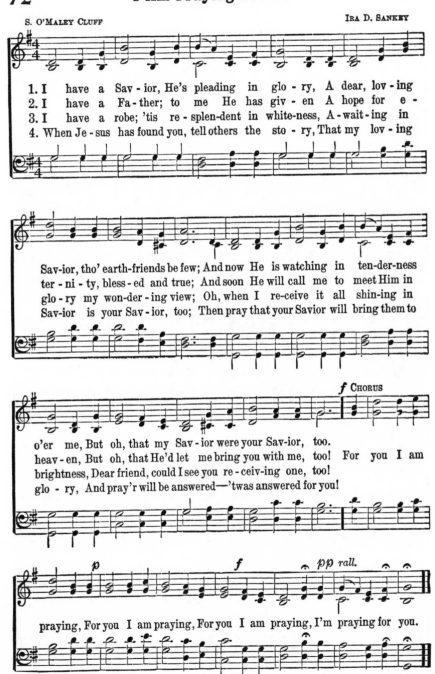

1. I have a Sav-ior, He's pleading in glo-ry, A dear, lov-ing
2. I have a Fa-ther; to me He has giv-en A hope for e-
3. I have a robe; 'tis re-splen-dent in white-ness, A-wait-ing in
4. When Je-sus has found you, tell others the sto-ry, That my lov-ing

Sav-ior, tho' earth-friends be few; And now He is watching in ten-der-ness
ter-ni-ty, bless-ed and true; And soon He will call me to meet Him in
glo-ry my won-der-ing view; Oh, when I re-ceive it all shin-ing in
Sav-ior is your Sav-ior, too; Then pray that your Savior will bring them to

f CHORUS

o'er me, But oh, that my Sav-ior were your Sav-ior, too.
heav-en, But oh, that He'd let me bring you with me, too! For you I am
brightness, Dear friend, could I see you re-ceiv-ing one, too!
glo-ry, And pray'r will be answered—'twas answered for you!

p   *f*   *pp rall.*

praying, For you I am praying, For you I am praying, I'm praying for you.

73 Love Lifted Me

JAMES ROWE

HOWARD E. SMITH

1. I was sink-ing deep in sin, Far from the peaceful shore, Ver - y deep-ly
2. All my heart to Him I give, Ev - er to Him I'll cling, In His bless-ed
3. Souls in dan-ger, look a-bove, Je - sus com-plete-ly saves; He will lift you

stained with-in, Sink-ing to rise no more; But the Mas - ter of the sea
pres - ence live, Ev - er His prais - es sing. Love so might-y and so true
by His love Out of the an - gry waves. He's the Mas - ter of the sea,

Heard my despairing cry, From the wa-ters lift - ed me, Now safe am I.
Mer-its my soul's best songs; Faith-ful, lov-ing serv-ice, too, To Him be - longs.
Bil-lows His will o - bey; He your Sav-ior wants to be—Be saved to - day.

CHORUS

Love lift-ed me!.... Love lift-ed me!.... When noth-ing
e - ven me! e - ven me!

1.
else could help, Love lift - ed me. 2. Love lift - ed me.

74 There is Power in the Blood

L. E. J.

L. E. JONES

1. Would you be free from the bur-den of sin? There's pow'r in the blood,
2. Would you be free from your pas-sion and pride? There's pow'r in the blood,
3. Would you be whit-er, much whiter than snow? There's pow'r in the blood,
4. Would you do serv-ice for Je-sus your King? There's pow'r in the blood,

pow'r in the blood; Would you o'er e-vil a vic-to-ry win? There's
pow'r in the blood; Come for a cleans-ing to Cal-va-ry's tide; There's
pow'r in the blood; Sin-stains are lost in its life-giv-ing flow; There's
pow'r in the blood; Would you live dai-ly His prais-es to sing? There's

CHORUS.

won-der-ful pow'r in the blood. There is pow'r, pow'r, Wonder-working pow'r
there is

In the blood of the Lamb; There is pow'r, pow'r,
In the blood of the Lamb; there is

Won-der-work-ing pow'r In the pre-cious blood of the Lamb.

75 Throw Out the Life-Line

EDWARD S. UFFORD

E. S. U. Arr. by GEO. C. STEBBINS

1. Throw out the Life-Line a-cross the dark wave, There is a broth-er whom some one should save; Some-bod-y's broth-er! oh, who then will dare To throw out the Life-Line, his per-il to share?

2. Throw out the Life-Line with hand quick and strong: Why do you tar-ry, why lin-ger so long? See! he is sink-ing; oh, has-ten to-day—And out with the Life-Boat! a-way, then, a-way! Throw out the Life-Line!

3. Throw out the Life-Line to dan-ger-fraught men, Sink-ing in an-guish where you've nev-er been: Winds of temp-ta-tion and bil-lows of woe Will soon hurl them out where the dark wa-ters flow.

4. Soon will the sea-son of res-cue be o'er, Soon will they drift to e-ter-ni-ty's shore, Haste then, my broth-er, no time for de-lay, But throw out the Life-Line and save them to-day.

CHORUS

Throw out the Life-Line! Some-one is drift-ing a-way; Throw out the Life-Line! Throw out the Life-Line! Some one is sink-ing to-day.

76　The Rock That is Higher Than I

E. JOHNSON

WILLIAM G. FISCHER

1. O some-times the shadows are deep, And rough seems the path to the goal,
2. O sometimes how long seems the day, And sometimes how wea-ry my feet;
3. O near to the Rock let me keep, If bless-ings or sor-rows pre-vail;

And sorrows, sometimes how they sweep Like tempests down o - ver the soul!
But toil - ing in life's dust-y way, The Rock's blessed shadow, how sweet!
Or climb-ing the mountain way steep, Or walk-ing the shad-ow-y vale.

REFRAIN

O then to the Rock let me fly, let me fly, To the

Rock that is high - er than I; is high - er than I; O then to the

Rock let me fly, let me fly, To the Rock that is high - er than I!

77   # When the Roll is Called Up Yonder

J. M. B.

J. M. BLACK

1. When the trumpet of the Lord shall sound, and time shall be no more, And the
2. On that bright and cloudless morning when the dead in Christ shall rise, And the
3. Let us la-bor for the Mas-ter from the dawn till set-ting sun, Let us

morning breaks, e-ter-nal, bright and fair; When the saved of earth shall gather
glo-ry of His res-ur-rec-tion share; When His cho-sen ones shall gather
talk of all His wondrous love and care; Then when all of life is o-ver,

o-ver on the oth-er shore, And the roll is called up yonder, I'll be there.
to their home beyond the skies, And the roll is called up yonder, I'll be there.
and our work on earth is done, And the roll is called up yonder, I'll be there.

FINE

D. S.—*roll is called up yonder, I'll be there.*

CHORUS

When the roll . . is called up yon - der, When the roll . . is called up
When the roll is called up yonder, I'll be there,   When the roll is called up

yon - - - der, When the roll . . . is called up yon - der, When the
yon - der, I'll be there,   When the roll is called up yon - der,

D. S.

78 The Way of the Cross Leads Home

JESSIE BROWN POUNDS

CHAS. H. GABRIEL

1. I must needs go home by the way of the cross, There's no oth-er
2. I must needs go on in the blood-sprinkled way, The path that the
3. Then I bid fare-well to the way of the world, To walk in it

way but this; I shall ne'er get sight of the Gates of Light,
Sav-ior trod, If I ev-er climb to the heights sub-lime,
nev-er-more; For my Lord says "Come," and I seek my home,

If the way of the cross I miss.
Where the soul is at home with God.
Where He waits at the o-pen door.

CHORUS.

The way of the cross leads home, The way of the cross leads home; It is
leads home, leads home;

sweet to know, as I on-ward go, The way of the cross leads home. A-MEN.

79 I Need Jesus

GEORGE O. WEBSTER

CHAS. H. GABRIEL

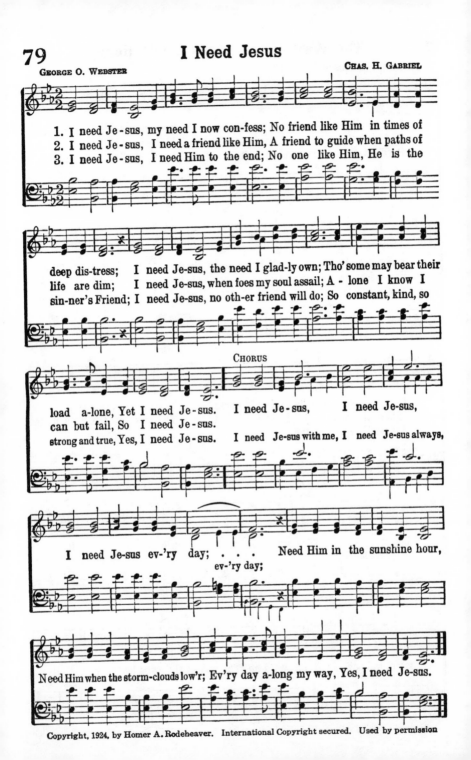

1. I need Je-sus, my need I now con-fess; No friend like Him in times of
2. I need Je-sus, I need a friend like Him, A friend to guide when paths of
3. I need Je-sus, I need Him to the end; No one like Him, He is the

deep dis-tress; I need Je-sus, the need I glad-ly own; Tho' some may bear their
life are dim; I need Je-sus, when foes my soul assail; A - lone I know I
sin-ner's Friend; I need Je-sus, no oth-er friend will do; So constant, kind, so

CHORUS

load a-lone, Yet I need Je-sus. I need Je-sus, I need Je-sus,
can but fail, So I need Je-sus.
strong and true, Yes, I need Je-sus. I need Je-sus with me, I need Je-sus always,

I need Je-sus ev-'ry day; . . . Need Him in the sunshine hour,
ev-'ry day;

Need Him when the storm-clouds low'r; Ev'ry day a-long my way, Yes, I need Je-sus.

80 There'll Be No Dark Valley

WILLIAM O. CUSHING

IRA D. SANKEY

1. There'll be no dark val-ley when Je-sus comes, There'll be no dark
2. There'll be no more sor-row when Je-sus comes, There'll be no more
3. There'll be no more weep-ing when Je-sus comes, There'll be no more
4. There'll be songs of greet-ing when Je-sus comes, There'll be songs of

val-ley when Je-sus comes; There'll be no dark val-ley when Je-sus comes
sor-row when Je-sus comes; But a glo-rious mor-row when Je-sus comes
weep-ing when Je-sus comes; But a bless-ed reap-ing when Je-sus comes
greet-ing when Je-sus comes; And a joy-ful meet-ing when Je-sus comes

REFRAIN

To gath-er His loved ones home. To gath-er His loved ones

home, (safe home,) To gath-er His loved ones home; (safe home;) There'll be

no dark val-ley when Je-sus comes To gath-er His loved ones home.

81 Christ Receiveth Sinful Men

Arr. from NEUMASTER, 1671

JAMES McGRANAHAN

1. Sin - ners Je - sus will re - ceive; Sound this word of grace to all
2. Come, and He will give you rest; Trust Him, for His word is plain;
3. Now my heart con-demns me not, Pure be - fore the law I stand;
4. Christ re - ceiv - eth sin - ful men, E - ven me with all my sin;

Who the heav'n - ly path-way leave, All who lin - ger, all who fall.
He will take the sin - ful - est; Christ re - ceiv - eth sin - ful men.
He who cleansed me from all spot, Sat - is - fied its last de-mand.
Purged from ev - 'ry spot and stain, Heav'n with Him I en - ter in.

REFRAIN

Sing it o'er . . . . . and o'er a - gain; . . . . . Christ re-
Sing it o'er a-gain,   Sing it o'er a - gain; Christ re-

ceiv - - - eth sin-ful men; . . . . . Make the mes - - - sage
ceiv-eth sin-ful men, Christ re-ceiv-eth sin - ful men; Make the message plain,

clear and plain: . . . . . . Christ re - ceiv - eth sin - ful men.
Make the mes-sage plain:

82 Sweet By and By

S. F. BENNETT

J. P. WEBSTER

1. There's a land that is fair - er than day, And by faith we can
2. We shall sing on that beau - ti - ful shore The mel - o - di - ous
3. To our boun - ti - ful Fa - ther a - bove, We will of - fer our

see it a - far; For the Fa - ther waits o - ver the way, To pre-
songs of the blest, And our spir - its shall sor - row no more, Not a
trib - ute of praise, For the glo - ri - ous gift of His love, And the

Chorus

pare us a dwell - ing-place there. In the sweet by and
sigh for the bless - ing of rest.
bless-ings that hal - low our days. In the sweet

by, We shall meet on that beau - ti - ful shore; In the
by and by, by and by,

sweet by and by, We shall meet on that beau - ti - ful shore.
In the sweet by and by,

83 Holy Quietness

M. P. FERGUSON

Arr. from W. S. MARSHALL

1. Joys are flow-ing like a riv - er, Since the Com-fort - er has come;
2. Spring-ing in - to life and gladness, All a-round this glorious Guest,
3. Like a rain that falls from heav-en, Like the sun-light from the sky,
4. What a won-der - ful sal - va - tion, Where we al - ways see His face!

He a - bides with us for - ev - er, Makes the trust-ing heart His home.
Ban-ished un - be - lief and sad-ness, And we just o - bey and trust.
So the Ho - ly Ghost is giv - en, Com - ing on us from on high.
What a peaceful hab - i - ta - tion, What a qui - et rest-ing place.

CHORUS

Blessed qui - et-ness, ho - ly qui-et-ness, What as - sur-ance in my soul;

On the storm-y sea, Speaking peace to me, How the bil-lows cease to roll.

84 The Ninety and Nine

Elizabeth C. Clephane

Ira D. Sankey

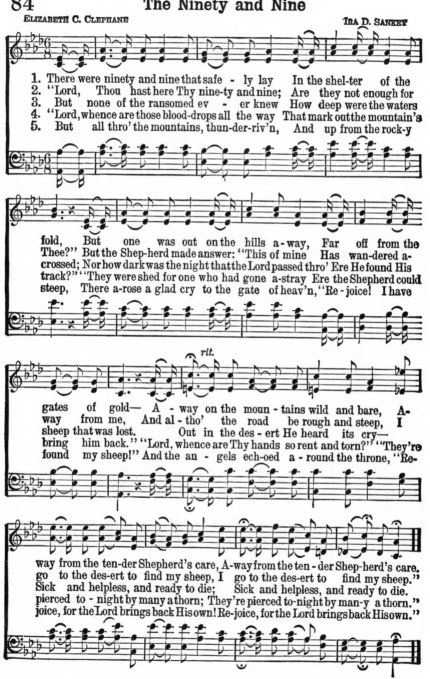

1. There were ninety and nine that safe - ly lay In the shel-ter of the
2. "Lord, Thou hast here Thy nine-ty and nine; Are they not enough for
3. But none of the ransomed ev - er knew How deep were the waters
4. "Lord, whence are those blood-drops all the way That mark out the mountain's
5. But all thro' the mountains, thun-der-riv'n, And up from the rock-y

fold, But one was out on the hills a - way, Far off from the
Thee?" But the Shep-herd made answer: "This of mine Has wan-dered a-
crossed; Nor how dark was the night that the Lord passed thro' Ere He found His
track?" "They were shed for one who had gone a-stray Ere the Shepherd could
steep, There a-rose a glad cry to the gate of heav'n, "Re - joice! I have

rit.

gates of gold— A - way on the moun - tains wild and bare, A-
way from me, And al - tho' the road be rough and steep, I
sheep that was lost. Out in the des - ert He heard its cry—
bring him back." "Lord, whence are Thy hands so rent and torn?" "They're
found my sheep!" And the an - gels ech-oed a - round the throne, "Re-

way from the ten-der Shepherd's care, A-way from the ten - der Shep-herd's care.
go to the des-ert to find my sheep, I go to the des-ert to find my sheep."
Sick and helpless, and ready to die; Sick and helpless, and ready to die.
pierced to - night by many a thorn; They're pierced to-night by man-y a thorn."
joice, for the Lord brings back His own! Re-joice, for the Lord brings back His own."

85   Grace Greater Than Our Sins

JULIA H. JOHNSTON   D. B. TOWNER

1. Mar - vel-ous grace of our lov - ing Lord, Grace that ex - ceeds our
2. Sin and de - spair like the sea waves cold, Threat-en the soul with
3. Dark is the stain that we can - not hide, What can a - vail to
4. Mar - vel-ous, in - fi - nite, match-less grace, Free - ly be - stowed on

sin and our guilt, Yon - der on Cal - va - ry's mount out - poured,
in - fi - nite loss; Grace that is great - er, yes, grace un - told,
wash it a - way? Look! there is flow - ing a crim - son tide;
all who be - lieve; You that are long - ing to see His face,

CHORUS

There where the blood of the Lamb was spilt.
Points to the Ref - uge, the Might - y Cross. Grace, grace,
Whit - er than snow you may be to - day.
Will you this mo - ment His grace re - ceive? Mar - vel - ous grace,

God's grace, Grace that will par-don and cleanse with-in; Grace,
In - fi - nite grace,   Mar - vel-ous

grace, God's grace, Grace that is great-er than all our sin.
grace, In - fi - nite grace,

86 In My Father's House Are Many Mansions

Arr. by Mrs. H. P. Armstrong

1. Come, Thou Fount of ev - 'ry bless - ing, Tune my heart to sing Thy grace;
2. Here I raise my Eb - en - e - zer, Hith - er by Thy help I'm come;
3. O to grace how great a debt - or Dai - ly I'm constrained to be!

Streams of mer - cy, nev - er ceas - ing, Call for songs of loud-est praise.
And I hope, by Thy good pleas-ure, Safe - ly to ar - rive at home.
Let Thy good-ness, like a fet - ter, Bind my wand'ring heart to Thee.

Chorus

"In My Fa - ther's house are man - y man - sions, If it

were not so I would have told you; In My Fa - ther's

rit.

house are man - y man-sions," And all the streets are paved with gold.

87   We're Marching to Zion

ISAAC WATTS   ROBERT LOWRY

Spirited

1. Come, we that love the Lord, And let our joys be known, Join in a song with sweet ac-cord, Join in a song with sweet ac-cord, And thus sur-round the throne, And thus sur-round the throne.

2. Let those re-fuse to sing Who nev-er knew our God; But chil-dren of the heav'n-ly King, But chil-dren of the heav'n-ly King, May speak their joys a-broad, May speak their joys a-broad.

3. The hill of Zi-on yields A thou-sand sa-cred sweets Be-fore we reach the heav'n-ly fields, Be-fore we reach the heav'n-ly fields, Or walk the gold-en streets, Or walk the gold-en streets.

4. Then let our songs a-bound, And ev-'ry tear be dry; We're marching thro' Immanuel's ground, We're marching thro' Immanuel's ground, To fair-er worlds on high, To fair-er worlds on high.

thus sur-round the throne, And thus sur-round the throne.

CHORUS

We're march-ing to Zi-on, Beau-ti-ful, beau-ti-ful Zi-on; We're

We're march-ing on to Zi-on,

march-ing up-ward to Zi-on, The beau-ti-ful cit-y of God.

Zi-on, Zi-on,

88 O That Will Be Glory

C. H. G.

CHAS. H. GABRIEL.

1. When all my la-bors and tri-als are o'er, And I am safe on that
2. When, by the gift of His in-fi-nite grace, I am ac-cord-ed in
3. Friends will be there I have loved long a-go; Joy like a riv-er a-

beau-ti-ful shore, Just to be near the dear Lord I a-dore,
Heav-en a place, Just to be there and to look on His face,
round me will flow; Yet, just a smile from my Sav-ior, I know,

rit. CHORUS. *Faster*

Will thro' the a-ges be glo-ry for me.... O that will be
O ...... that will

glo-ry for me, Glo-ry for me, glo-ry for me; When by His grace
be glo-ry for me, Glo-ry for me, glo-ry for me;......

rit.

I shall look on His face, That will be glo-ry, be glo-ry for me.

89 I Must Tell Jesus

E. A. H.

E. A. HOFFMAN

1. I must tell Je-sus all of my tri-als; I can-not bear these
2. I must tell Je-sus all of my troub-les; He is a kind, com-
3. Tempted and tried I need a great Sav-ior, One who can help my
4. O how the world to e-vil al-lures me! O how my heart is

bur-dens a-lone; In my dis-tress He kind-ly will help me;
pas-sion-ate Friend; If I but ask Him, He will de-liv-er,
bur-dens to bear; I must tell Je-sus, I must tell Je-sus;
tempt-ed to sin! I must tell Je-sus, and He will help me

CHORUS

He ev-er loves and cares for His own. I must tell Je-sus!
Make of my troub-les quick-ly an end.
He all my cares and sor-rows will share.
O-ver the world the vic-t'ry to win.

I must tell Je-sus! I can-not bear my bur-dens a-lone; I must tell

Je-sus! I must tell Je-sus! Je-sus can help me, Je-sus a-lone.

90 Wonderful Peace

W. D. CORNELL. Alt.

W. G. COOPER

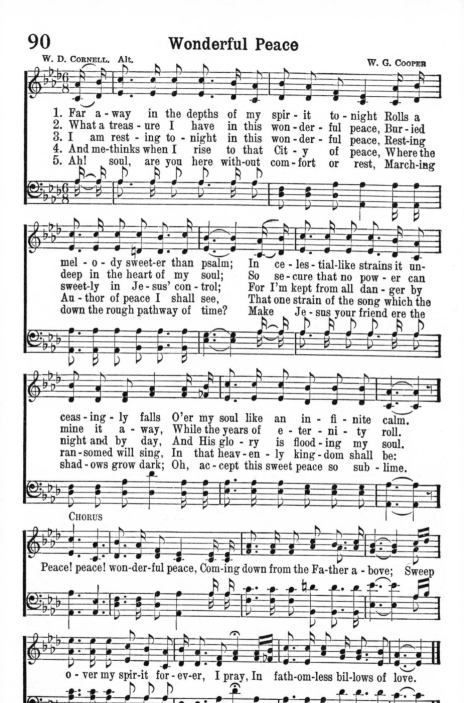

1. Far a - way in the depths of my spir - it to - night Rolls a
2. What a treas - ure I have in this won - der - ful peace, Bur - ied
3. I am rest - ing to - night in this won - der - ful peace, Rest - ing
4. And me-thinks when I rise to that Cit - y of peace, Where the
5. Ah! soul, are you here with-out com - fort or rest, March-ing

mel - o - dy sweet-er than psalm; In ce - les - tial-like strains it un-
deep in the heart of my soul; So se - cure that no pow - er can
sweet-ly in Je - sus' con - trol; For I'm kept from all dan - ger by
Au - thor of peace I shall see, That one strain of the song which the
down the rough pathway of time? Make Je - sus your friend ere the

ceas - ing - ly falls O'er my soul like an in - fi - nite calm.
mine it a - way, While the years of e - ter - ni - ty roll.
night and by day, And His glo - ry is flood - ing my soul.
ran - somed will sing, In that heav - en - ly king - dom shall be:
shad - ows grow dark; Oh, ac - cept this sweet peace so sub - lime.

CHORUS

Peace! peace! won-der-ful peace, Com-ing down from the Fa - ther a - bove; Sweep

o - ver my spir-it for - ev-er, I pray, In fath-om-less bil-lows of love.

91 The Old Rugged Cross

REV. GEO. BENNARD   REV. GEO. BENNARD

1. On a hill far a - way stood an old rugged cross, The emblem of
2. Oh, that old rugged cross, so despised by the world, Has a wondrous at -
3. In the old rugged cross, stained with blood so di-vine, A won - drous
4. To the old rugged cross I will ev - er be true, Its shame and re -

suf - f'ring and shame; And I love that old cross where the dear - est and best
trac - tion for me; For the dear Lamb of God left His glo - ry a - bove
beau - ty I see; For 'twas on that old cross Je - sus suf - fered and died
proach glad-ly bear; Then He'll call me some day to my home far a - way,

CHORUS.

For a world of lost sin-ners was slain. So I'll cher-ish the old rug-ged
To bear it to dark Cal - va - ry.
To par - don and sanc-ti - fy me.
Where His glo - ry for - ev - er I'll share.   cross, the

cross, ... Till my tro-phies at last I lay down; I will cling to the
old rug-ged cross,

old rug-ged cross, ... And exchange it some day for a crown.
cross, the old rugged cross,

92 The Lily of the Valley

English Melody

1. I have found a friend in Je - sus, He's ev - 'ry - thing to me, He's the
2. He all my grief has tak - en, and all my sor - rows borne; In temp -
3. He will nev - er, nev - er leave me, nor yet for - sake me here, While I

fair - est of ten thou - sand to my soul; The Lil - y of the Val - ley, in
ta - tion He's my strong and mighty tow'r; I have all for Him for - sak - en, and
live by faith and do His bless - ed will; A wall of fire a - bout me, I've

D. S.—Lil - y of the Val - ley, the

Him a - lone I see All I need to cleanse and make me ful - ly whole.
all my i - dols torn From my heart, and now He keeps me by His pow'r.
noth - ing now to fear, With His man - na He my hun - gry soul shall fill.

bright and Morn - ing Star, He's the fair - est of ten thou - sand to my soul.

In sor - row He's my com - fort, in troub - le He's my stay,
Though all the world for - sake me, and Sa - tan tempts me sore,
Then sweep - ing up to glo - ry, to see His bless - ed face,

He tells me ev - 'ry care on Him to roll. He's the
Through Je - sus I shall safe - ly reach the goal; He's the
Where riv - ers of de - light shall ev - er roll! He's the
Hal - le - lu - jah!

93 Let Jesus Come Into Your Heart

C. H. M.

Mrs. C. H. Morris

1. If you are tired of the load of your sin, Let Je - sus come in - to your heart;
2. If 'tis for pu - ri - ty now that you sigh, Let Je - sus come in - to your heart;
3. If there's a tem - pest your voice can - not still, Let Je - sus come in - to your heart;
4. If you would join the glad songs of the blest, Let Je - sus come in - to your heart;

If you de - sire a new life to be - gin,
Fountains for cleans-ing are flow-ing near by,
If there's a void this world nev - er can fill,
If you would en - ter the man-sions of rest,

Let Je - sus come in - to your heart.

CHORUS

Just now, your doubt-ings give o'er; Just now, re - ject Him no more; Just now, throw o - pen the door; Let Je - sus come in - to your heart.

94 Jesus Saves

PRISCILLA J. OWENS

WM. J. KIRKPATRICK

1. We have heard the joy-ful sound: Je-sus saves! Je-sus saves!
2. Waft it on the roll-ing tide; Je-sus saves! Je-sus saves!
3. Sing a-bove the bat-tle strife, Je-sus saves! Je-sus saves!
4. Give the winds a might-y voice, Je-sus saves! Je-sus saves!

Spread the ti-dings all a-round: Je-sus saves! Je-sus saves!
Tell to sin-ners far and wide: Je-sus saves! Je-sus saves!
By His death and end-less life, Je-sus saves! Je-sus saves!
Let the na-tions now re-joice,— Je-sus saves! Je-sus saves!

Bear the news to ev-'ry land, Climb the steeps and cross the waves;
Sing, ye is-lands of the sea; Ech-o back, ye o-cean caves;
Sing it soft-ly thro' the gloom, When the heart for mer-cy craves;
Shout sal-va-tion full and free; High-est hills and deep-est caves;

On-ward!—'tis our Lord's com-mand; Je-sus saves! Je-sus saves!
Earth shall keep her ju-bi-lee: Je-sus saves! Je-sus saves!
Sing in tri-umph o'er the tomb,— Je-sus saves! Je-sus saves!
This our song of vic-to-ry,— Je-sus saves! Je-sus saves!

95 The Home Over There

D. W. C. Huntington

Tullius C. O'Kane

1. O think of the home o-ver there, By the side of the riv-er of
2. O think of the friends o-ver there, Who be-fore us the jour-ney have
3. My Sav-ior is now o-ver there, There my kin-dred and friends are at
4. I'll soon be at home o-ver there, For the end of my jour-ney I

light,   Where the saints, all im-mor-tal and fair,   Are
trod,   Of the songs that they breathe on the air,   In their
rest;   Then a-way from my sor-row and care,   Let me
see;   Man-y dear to my heart, o-ver there,   Are

o - ver there,

robed in their garments of white,   O - ver there,   o - ver
home in the pal-ace of God.   O - ver there,   o - ver
fly   to the land of the blest.   O - ver there,   o - ver
watch-ing and wait-ing for me.   O - ver there,   o - ver

o - ver there.

REFRAIN.

O - ver there,

there,   O think of the home o - ver there,   O - ver
there,   O think of the friends o - ver there,   O - ver
there,   My Sav - ior is now o - ver there,   O - ver
there,   I'll soon be at home o - ver there,   O - ver

o - ver there,   o - ver there,

The Home Over There

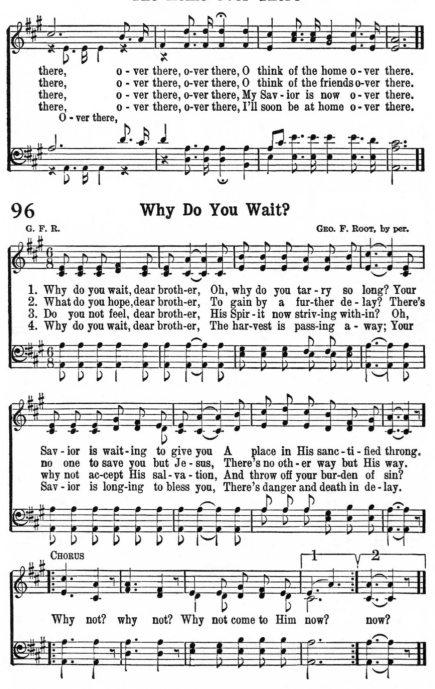

there,   o - ver there, o-ver there, O think of the home o - ver there.
there,   o - ver there, o-ver there, O think of the friends o-ver there.
there,   o - ver there, o-ver there, My Sav - ior is now o - ver there.
there,   o - ver there, o-ver there, I'll soon be at home o - ver there.
        O - ver there,

96 Why Do You Wait?

G. F. R.

GEO. F. ROOT, by per.

1. Why do you wait, dear broth-er, Oh, why do you tar - ry so long? Your
2. What do you hope, dear broth-er, To gain by a fur-ther de - lay? There's
3. Do you not feel, dear broth-er, His Spir - it now striv-ing with-in? Oh,
4. Why do you wait, dear broth-er, The har-vest is pass-ing a - way; Your

Sav - ior is wait-ing to give you A   place in His sanc-ti -fied throng.
no one to save you but Je - sus, There's no oth - er way but His way.
why not ac-cept His sal - va - tion, And throw off your bur-den of sin?
Sav - ior is long-ing to bless you, There's danger and death in de - lay.

CHORUS

Why not? why   not? Why not come to Him now?   now?

97 Loved By the King

JAMES ROWE

JAMES V. REID

1. My life was a fail-ure, for I was a-stray, And serv-ing the
2. The world could not help me, all friends I had lost, A - lone and in
3. O soul, lost in dark-ness, my King is the Lord, Who al - so for

tempt - er from day un - to day; But now, home-ward go - ing, a
sor - row, by bil - lows was tossed; But now I have Some-One to
you has His life - blood out-poured; So ask - ing for - give - ness, your

rit.

glad song I sing, For I am for - giv - en and loved by the King.
whom I may cling, And look to in troub-le,—I'm loved by the King.
heart to Him bring, That you may for - ev - er be loved by the King.

CHORUS

I'm loved by the King, He redeemed me, His prais-es re-joic-ing I sing; I'm

tempo *rit.*

lonely no more, my wand'rings are o'er, I'm loved by the King, hal-le-lu-jah! A-MEN.

98 The Christ of the Cross

Tune: "The Church in the Wildwood"

M. L. ARMSTRONG

Dr. WILLIAM S. PITTS

1. There is One who was sent here to save you, His life's blood was shed on the cross, He paid the price of for-give-ness, Oh, come to the Christ of the cross.

2. Oh, come to the Sav-ior of sin-ners, For He is tru-ly your friend, And God who loves all so dear-ly, His Son to re-deem you did send.

3. You may have lived ver-y care-less, From right hav-ing wan-dered a-way, But re-mem-ber that Christ is your Sav-ior, Oh, come and ac-cept Him to-day?

[D. S.—*No one ev-er loved you so dear-ly As this Sav-ior who died on the cross.*

FINE. CHORUS

Come to the Sav-ior of sin-ners, Oh, come to the Christ of the cross;

Oh, come, come, come, come, come, come, come, come, come, come, come, come, come, come, come, come, come;

D. S.

99 Lead Me Gently Home, Father

W. L. T.

W. L. THOMPSON

Solo or Duet. *ad lib.*

1. Lead me gen-tly home, Fa-ther, Lead me gen-tly home, When life's toils are
2. Lead me gen-tly home, Fa-ther, Lead me gen-tly home, In life's dark-est

end - ed, And part-ing days have come; Sin no more shall tempt me, Ne'er from
hours, Father, When life's troubles come; Keep my feet from wand'ring, Lest from

rit. *p*

Thee I'll roam, If Thou'lt on - ly lead me, Fa-ther, Lead me gen-tly home.
Thee I roam, Lest I fall up - on the way-side, Lead me gen-tly home.

REFRAIN

Lead me gen - tly home, Fa - ther, Lead me gen - tly,
Lead me gen - tly home, Fa - ther, Lead me gen - tly home, Fa - ther,

Lest I fall up - on the way - side, Lead me gen - tly home.
gen - tly home.

100 I Love To Tell The Story

KATHERINE HANKEY

WILLIAM G. FISCHER

1. I love to tell the sto - ry Of un - seen things a - bove, Of Je - sus
2. I love to tell the sto - ry; More won-der - ful it seems Than all the
3. I love to tell the sto - ry; 'Tis pleas-ant to re - peat What seems each
4. I love to tell the sto - ry; For those who know it best Seem hun-ger-

and His glo - ry, Of Je - sus and His love, I love to tell the sto - ry,
gold - en fan-cies Of all my golden dreams. I love to tell the sto - ry;
time I tell it, More won-der-ful - ly sweet. I love to tell the sto - ry;
ing and thirsting To hear it like the rest. And when, in scenes of glo - ry,

Because I know 'tis true, It sat - is-fies my longings, As nothing else can do.
It did so much for me; And that is just the rea-son I tell it now to thee
For some have never heard The message of salvation From God's own holy word.
I sing the new, new song, 'Twill be the old, old story, That I have loved so long.

CHORUS

I love to tell the sto - ry! 'Twill be my theme in glo - ry

To tell the old, old sto - ry Of Je - sus and His love.

Blessed Assurance

Fanny J. Crosby

Mrs. J. F. Knapp

1. Bless-ed as-sur-ance, Je-sus is mine! Oh, what a fore-taste of
2. Per-fect sub-mis-sion, per-fect de-light, Vi-sions of rap-ture now
3. Per-fect sub-mis-sion, all is at rest, I in my Sav-ior am

glo-ry di-vine! Heir of sal-va-tion, pur-chase of God,
burst on my sight; An-gels de-scend-ing, bring from a-bove
hap-py and blest; Watching and wait-ing, look-ing a-bove,

CHORUS

Born of His Spir-it, washed in His blood.
Ech-oes of mer-cy, whis-pers of love. This is my sto-ry, this is my
Filled with His goodness, lost in His love.

song, Prais-ing my Sav-ior all the day long; This is my sto-ry,

this is my song, Prais-ing my Sav-ior all the day long.

102 Jesus Is Calling

FANNY J. CROSBY

GEO. C. STEBBINS

1. Je-sus is ten-der-ly call-ing thee home—Call-ing to-day, call-ing to-day; Why from the sun-shine of love wilt thou roam Far-ther and far-ther a-way?
2. Je-sus is call-ing the wea-ry to rest—Call-ing to-day, call-ing to-day; Bring Him thy bur-den and thou shalt be blest: He will not turn thee a-way.
3. Je-sus is wait-ing; O come to Him now—Wait-ing to-day, wait-ing to-day; Come with thy sins; at His feet low-ly bow; Come, and no lon-ger de-lay.
4. Je-sus is plead-ing; O list to His voice: Hear Him to-day, hear Him to-day; They who be-lieve on His name shall re-joice; Quick-ly a-rise and a-way.

REFRAIN

Call - - ing to-day, ... Call - - ing to-day, ... Je - - - sus is call - - - ing, is ten-der-ly call-ing to-day.

Call-ing, call-ing to-day, to-day, Call-ing, call-ing to-day, to-day, Je-sus is ten-der-ly call-ing to-day,

I Am Thine, O Lord

FANNY J. CROSBY

W. H. DOANE

1. I am Thine, O Lord, I have heard Thy voice, And it told Thy love to me; But I long to rise in the arms of faith, And be clos-er drawn to Thee.

2. Con-se-crate me now to Thy serv-ice, Lord, By the pow'r of grace di-vine; Let my soul look up with a stead-fast hope, And my will be lost in Thine.

3. O the pure de-light of a sin-gle hour That be-fore Thy throne I spend, When I kneel in prayer, and with Thee, my God, I com-mune as friend with friend!

4. There are depths of love that I can-not know Till I cross the nar-row sea; There are heights of joy that I may not reach Till I rest in peace with Thee.

REFRAIN

Draw me near - er, near-er, bless-ed Lord, To the cross where Thou hast died; Draw me near-er, near-er, near-er, bless-ed Lord, To Thy pre-cious, bleed-ing side.

near - er, near - er,

104 Is My Name Written There?

M. A. K.

FRANK M. DAVIS

1. Lord, I care not for rich-es, Nei-ther sil-ver nor gold; I would
2. Lord, my sins they are man-y, Like the sands of the sea, But Thy
3. Oh! that beau-ti-ful cit-y, With its man-sions of light, With its

make sure of heav-en, I would en-ter the fold. In the book of Thy
blood, O my Sav-ior, Is suf-fi-cient for me; For Thy prom-ise is
glo-ri-fied be-ings, In pure gar-ments of white; Where no e-vil thing

king-dom, With its pa-ges so fair, Tell me, Je-sus, my Sav-ior, Is my
writ-ten, In bright letters that glow, "Tho' your sins be as scar-let, I will
com-eth To de-spoil what is fair; Where the an-gels are watching, Yes, my

REFRAIN.

name writ-ten there?
make them like snow." Is my name writ-ten there, On the page white and fair?
name's written there. Yes, my name's, etc.

In the book of Thy king-dom, Is my name writ-ten there?
Yes, my name's writ-ten there.

105 Higher Ground

JOHNSON OATMAN, JR.

CHAS. H. GABRIEL

1. I'm press-ing on the up-ward way, New heights I'm gaining ev-'ry day;
2. My heart has no de-sire to stay Where doubts a-rise and fears dis-may;
3. I want to live a-bove the world, Tho' Sa-tan's darts at me are hurled;
4. I want to scale the utmost height, And catch a gleam of glo-ry bright;

Still pray-ing as I on-ward bound, "Lord, plant my feet on high-er ground."
Tho' some may dwell where these abound, My prayer, my aim, is high-er ground.
For faith has caught the joy-ful sound, The song of saints on high-er ground.
But still I'll pray till Heav'n I've found, "Lord, lead me on to high-er ground."

CHORUS

Lord, lift me up and let me stand, By faith, on Heav-en's ta-ble-land,

A high-er plane than I have found; Lord, plant my feet on high-er ground.

106 Softly and Tenderly

W. L. T.

WILL L. THOMPSON

1. Soft - ly and ten-der - ly Je - sus is call-ing, Call - ing for you and for me;
2. Why should we tarry when Jesus is plead-ing, Pleading for you and for me?
3. Time is now fleeting, the moments are passing, Passing from you and from me;
4. Oh! for the won-der-ful love He has promised, Promised for you and for me;

See, on the portals He's waiting and watching, Watching for you and for me.
Why should we linger and heed not His mercies, Mer-cies for you and for me?
Shadows are gathering, death-beds are coming, Com-ing for you and for me.
Tho' we have sinned, He has mercy and pardon, Par-don for you and for me.

CHORUS

Come home,... come home,...... Ye who are wear-y, come home;...
Come home, come home,

Ear-nest-ly, ten-der-ly, Je - sus is call-ing, Call-ing, O sin-ner, come home!

107 The Great Physician

WM. HUNTER

J. H. STOCKTON
FINE

1. {The great Phy-si-cian now is here, The sym-pa-thiz-ing Je-sus;}
   {He speaks the droop-ing heart to cheer, O hear the voice of Je-sus.}

2. {Your man-y sins are all for-giv'n, O hear the voice of Je-sus;}
   {Go on your way in peace to heav'n, And wear a crown with Je-sus.}

3. {All glo-ry to the dy-ing Lamb! I now be-lieve in Je-sus;}
   {I love the bless-ed Sav-ior's name, I love the name of Je-sus.}

4. {And when to that bright world a-bove, We rise to be with Je-sus,}
   {We'll sing a-round the throne of love, His name, the name of Je-sus.}

D. S.—*Sweet-est car-ol ev-er sung,* ⁊ *Je-sus, bless-ed Je-sus.*

REFRAIN

D. S.

Sweet-est note of ser-aph song, Sweet-est name on mor-tal tongue;

108 Revive Us Again

WM. P. MACKAY

JOHN J. HUSBAND

1. We praise Thee, O God! for the Son of Thy love, For Je-sus who
2. We praise Thee, O God! for Thy Spir-it of light, Who has shown us our
3. All glo-ry and praise to the Lamb that was slain, Who has borne all our
4. Re-vive us a-gain; fill each heart with Thy love; May each soul be re-

CHORUS

died, and is now gone a-bove.
Sav-ior, and scat-tered our night. Hal-le-lu-jah! Thine the glo-ry, Hal-le-
sins, and has cleansed ev-'ry stain.
kin-dled with fire from a-bove.

Revive Us Again

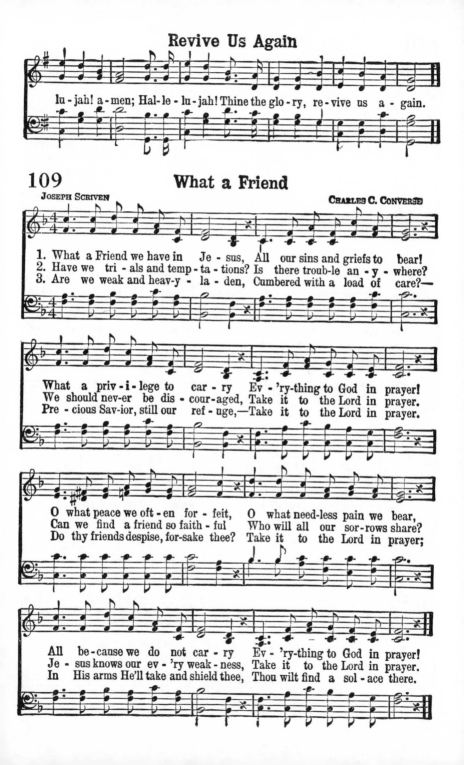

lu - jah! a - men; Hal- le - lu-jah! Thine the glo - ry, re - vive us a - gain.

109 What a Friend

JOSEPH SCRIVEN

CHARLES C. CONVERSE

1. What a Friend we have in Je - sus, All our sins and griefs to bear!
2. Have we tri - als and temp - ta - tions? Is there troub-le an - y - where?
3. Are we weak and heav-y - la - den, Cumbered with a load of care?—

What a priv - i - lege to car - ry Ev - 'ry-thing to God in prayer!
We should nev-er be dis - cour-aged, Take it to the Lord in prayer.
Pre - cious Sav-ior, still our ref - uge,—Take it to the Lord in prayer.

O what peace we oft - en for - feit, O what need-less pain we bear,
Can we find a friend so faith - ful Who will all our sor-rows share?
Do thy friends despise, for-sake thee? Take it to the Lord in prayer;

All be-cause we do not car - ry Ev - 'ry-thing to God in prayer!
Je - sus knows our ev - 'ry weak - ness, Take it to the Lord in prayer.
In His arms He'll take and shield thee, Thou wilt find a sol - ace there.

Whiter Than Snow

110

JAMES NICHOLSON

WM. G. FISCHER

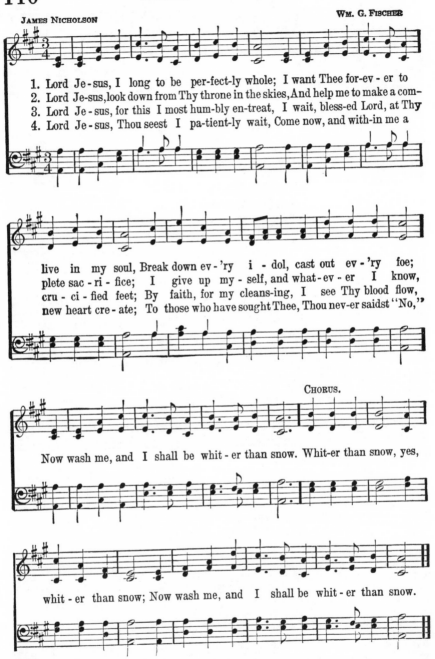

1. Lord Je-sus, I long to be per-fect-ly whole; I want Thee for-ev - er to
2. Lord Je-sus, look down from Thy throne in the skies, And help me to make a com-
3. Lord Je-sus, for this I most hum-bly en-treat, I wait, bless-ed Lord, at Thy
4. Lord Je-sus, Thou seest I pa-tient-ly wait, Come now, and with-in me a

live in my soul, Break down ev-'ry i - dol, cast out ev-'ry foe;
plete sac - ri - fice; I give up my - self, and what-ev - er I know,
cru - ci - fied feet; By faith, for my cleans-ing, I see Thy blood flow,
new heart cre - ate; To those who have sought Thee, Thou nev-er saidst "No,"

CHORUS.

Now wash me, and I shall be whit - er than snow. Whit-er than snow, yes,

whit - er than snow; Now wash me, and I shall be whit - er than snow.

111 My Hope Is Built

EDWARD MOTE

WILLIAM B. BRADBURY

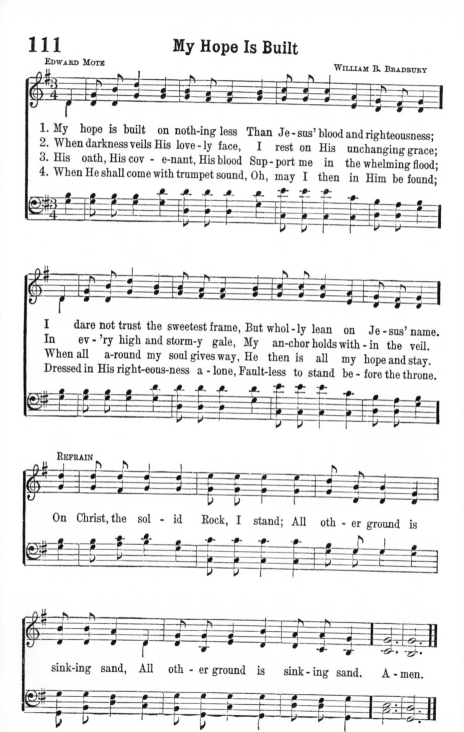

1. My hope is built on noth-ing less Than Je-sus' blood and righteousness;
2. When darkness veils His love-ly face, I rest on His unchanging grace;
3. His oath, His cov-e-nant, His blood Sup-port me in the whelming flood;
4. When He shall come with trumpet sound, Oh, may I then in Him be found;

I dare not trust the sweetest frame, But whol-ly lean on Je-sus' name.
In ev-'ry high and storm-y gale, My an-chor holds with-in the veil.
When all a-round my soul gives way, He then is all my hope and stay.
Dressed in His right-eous-ness a-lone, Fault-less to stand be-fore the throne.

REFRAIN

On Christ, the sol-id Rock, I stand; All oth-er ground is

sink-ing sand, All oth-er ground is sink-ing sand. A-men.

112 Almost Persuaded

P. P. B.

P. P. BLISS

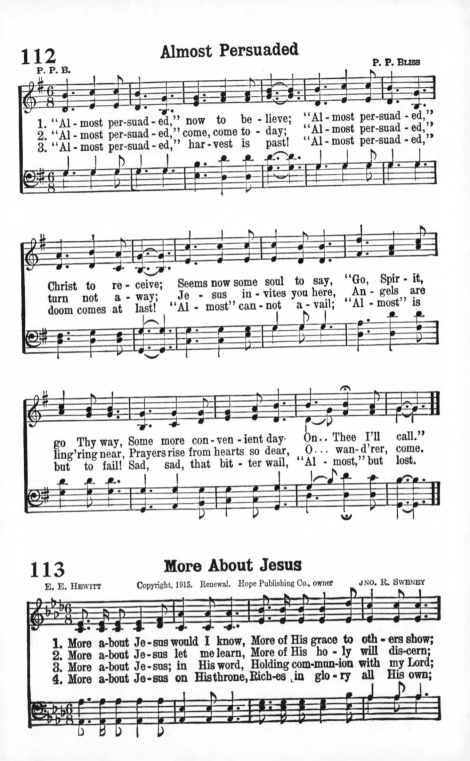

1. "Al - most per-suad - ed," now to be - lieve; "Al - most per-suad - ed,"
2. "Al - most per-suad - ed," come, come to - day; "Al - most per-suad - ed,"
3. "Al - most per-suad - ed," har - vest is past! "Al - most per-suad - ed,"

Christ to re - ceive; Seems now some soul to say, "Go, Spir - it,
turn not a - way; Je - sus in - vites you here, An - gels are
doom comes at last! "Al - most" can - not a - vail; "Al - most" is

go Thy way, Some more con - ven - ient day. On.. Thee I'll call."
ling'ring near, Prayers rise from hearts so dear, O... wan-d'rer, come.
but to fail! Sad, sad, that bit - ter wail, "Al - most," but lost.

113 More About Jesus

E. E. HEWITT

Copyright, 1915. Renewal. Hope Publishing Co., owner

JNO. R. SWENEY

1. More a-bout Je-sus would I know, More of His grace to oth - ers show;
2. More a-bout Je-sus let me learn, More of His ho - ly will dis-cern;
3. More a-bout Je-sus; in His word, Holding com-mun-ion with my Lord;
4. More a-bout Je-sus on His throne, Rich-es in glo - ry all His own;

More About Jesus

FINE

More of His sav-ing full-ness see, More of His love who died for me.
Spir-it of God, my teach-er be, Show-ing the things of Christ to me.
Hear-ing His voice in ev-'ry line, Mak-ing each faith-ful say-ing mine.
More of His kingdom's sure in-crease; More of His com-ing, Prince of Peace.

D.S.—*More of His sav-ing full-ness see, More of His love who died for me.*

REFRAIN

D.S.

More, more a-bout Je-sus, More, more a-bout Je-sus;

114 G. DUFFIELD Stand Up For Jesus G. J. WEBB

1. Stand up, stand up for Je-sus, Ye sol-diers of the cross, Lift high His
2. Stand up, stand up for Je-sus, The trump-et call o-bey; Forth to the
3. Stand up, stand up for Je-sus—Stand in His strength a-lone; The arm of

roy-al ban-ner, It must not suf-fer loss; From vic-t'ry un-to vic-t'ry, His
might-y con-flict, In this His glorious day. "Ye that are men now serve Him," A-
flesh will fail you—Ye dare not trust your own; Put on the gos-pel ar-mor, And,

ar-my shall He lead, Till ev-'ry foe is vanquished And Christ is Lord in-deed.
gainst unnumbered foes; Let courage rise with danger, And strength to strength oppose.
watching un-to prayer, Where duty calls, or dan-ger, Be nev-er want-ing there.

115 Near The Cross

FANNY J. CROSBY
W. H. DOANE

1. Je - sus, keep me near the cross, There a pre - cious foun - tain
2. Near the cross, a trem-bling soul, Love and mer - cy found me;
3. Near the cross! O Lamb of God, Bring its scenes be - fore me;
4. Near the cross I'll watch and wait, Hop - ing, trust-ing ev - er,

Free to all— a heal - ing stream, Flows from Cal-v'ry's moun - tain.
There the Bright and Morn - ing Star Sheds its beams a - round me.
Help me walk from day to day, With its shad - ows o'er me.
Till I reach the gold - en strand, Just be - yond the riv - er.

CHORUS

In the cross, in the cross, Be my glo - ry ev - er;

Till my rap-tured soul shall find Rest be - yond the riv - er.

116 Nearer, My God, to Thee

SARAH F. ADAMS
ARR. by LOWELL MASON

1. Near - er, my God, to Thee, Near - er to Thee! E'en though it
2. Though like the wan - der - er, The sun gone down, Dark - ness be
3. There let the way ap - pear, Steps un - to Heav'n: All that Thou
4. Then, with my wak - ing tho'ts Bright with Thy praise, Out of my
5. Or if on joy - ful wing, Cleav - ing the sky, Sun, moon, and

118 Bringing In the Sheaves

KNOWLES SHAW

GEORGE A. MINOR

1. Sow-ing in the morn-ing, sow-ing seeds of kind-ness, Sowing in the
2. Sow-ing in the sun-shine, sow-ing in the shad-ows, Fear-ing nei-ther
3. Go-ing forth with weep-ing, sow-ing for the Mas-ter, Tho' the loss sus-

noon-tide and the dew-y eve; Wait-ing for the har-vest,
clouds nor win-ter's chill-ing breeze; By and by the har-vest,
tained our spir-it oft-en grieves; When our weep-ing's o-ver,

and the time of reap-ing, We shall come re-joic-ing, bring-ing in the sheaves.
and the la-bor end-ed, We shall come re-joic-ing, bring-ing in the sheaves.
He will bid us wel-come, We shall come re-joic-ing, bring-ing in the sheaves.

CHORUS

Bring-ing in the sheaves, bring-ing in the sheaves, We shall come re-joic-
Bring-ing in the sheaves, bring-ing in the sheaves, We shall come re-joic-

1. ing, bring-ing in the sheaves; 2. ing, bring-ing in the sheaves.

119 Saved, Saved!

J. P. S.

J. P. Scholfield

1. I've found a friend who is all to me,.... His
2. He saves me from ev-'ry sin and harm,.. Se-
3. When poor and need-y and all a-lone,... In

love is ev-er true;...... I love to tell how He
cures my soul each day;...... I'm lean-ing strong on His
love He said to me,........ "Come un-to me and I'll

lift-ed me.... And what His grace can do for you...
might-y arm;.. I know He'll guide me all the way...
lead you home, To live with me e-ter-nal-ly."...

Chorus.

Saved .... by His pow'r di-vine, Saved .... to new life sub-lime!
Saved by His pow'r, Saved to new life,

Life now is sweet and my joy is com-plete, For I'm Saved, saved, saved!

120 More Love To Thee

ELIZABETH PRENTISS

W. H. DOANE

1. More love to Thee, O Christ, More love to Thee! Hear Thou the
2. Once earth-ly joy I craved, Sought peace and rest; Now Thee a -
3. Then shall my lat - est breath Whis - per Thy praise; This be the

pray'r I make On bend - ed knee; This is my earn - est plea:
lone I seek, Give what is best; This all my pray'r shall be:
part - ing cry My heart shall raise; This still its pray'r shall be:

More love, O Christ, to Thee, More love to Thee, More love to Thee!

121 I Am Coming, Lord

L. H.

Used by permission

L. HARTSOUGH

1. I hear Thy welcome voice, That calls me, Lord, to Thee, For cleansing in Thy
2. Tho' coming weak and vile, Thou dost my strength assure; Thou dost my vileness
3. 'Tis Je - sus calls me on To per - fect faith and love, To per - fect hope, and

CHORUS

pre-cious blood That flowed on Cal-va-ry.
full - y cleanse, Till spot-less all and pure.   I am coming, Lord! Coming now to
peace, and trust, For earth and Heav'n above.

I Am Coming, Lord

Thee! Wash me, cleanse me in the blood That flowed on Cal-va-ry!

122 Hold the Fort

P. P. B.

P. P. BLISS

1. Ho, my com-rades! see the sig-nal Wav-ing in the sky!
2. See the might-y host ad-vanc-ing, Sa-tan lead-ing on;
3. See the glo-rious ban-ner wav-ing! Hear the trump-et blow!
4. Fierce and long the bat-tle rag-es, But our help is near;

Re-in-force-ments now ap-pear-ing, Vic-to-ry is nigh.
Might-y men a-round us fall-ing, Cour-age al-most gone!
In our Lead-er's name we tri-umph O-ver ev-'ry foe.
On-ward comes our great Com-mand-er, Cheer, my com-rades, cheer!

CHORUS

"Hold the fort, for I am com-ing," Je-sus sig-nals still;

Wave the an-swer back to heav-en, "By Thy grace we will."

123 Jesus Savior, Pilot Me

Pilot 7s

EDWARD HOPPER

J. E. GOULD

FINE.

1. Je - sus, Sav - ior, pi - lot me O - ver life's tem - pes - tuous sea:
2. As a moth - er stills her child, Thou canst hush the o - cean wild;
3. When at last I near the shore, And the fear - ful break-ers roar

D. C.—Chart and com-pass come from Thee, Je - sus, Sav - ior, pi - lot me.
D. C.—Won-drous Sov-'reign of the sea, Je - sus, Sav - ior, pi - lot me.
D. C.—May I hear Thee say to me, "Fear not, I will pi - lot thee."

D. C.

Un-known waves be - fore me roll, Hid - ing rocks and treach'rous shoal;
Bois-t'rous waves o - bey Thy will When Thou say'st to them "Be still!"
'Twixt me and the peace-ful rest, Then, while lean-ing on Thy breast,

124 I Need Thee Every Hour

MRS. ANNIE S. HAWKS

REV. ROBERT LOWRY

1. I need Thee ev - 'ry hour, Most gra-cious Lord; No ten - der voice like
2. I need Thee ev - 'ry hour, Stay Thou near by; Temp-ta - tions lose their
3. I need Thee ev - 'ry hour, In joy or pain; Come quick-ly and a -
4. I need Thee ev - 'ry hour, Most Ho - ly One; O make me Thine in -

CHORUS

Thine Can peace af - ford.
pow'r When Thou art nigh. I need Thee, O I need Thee; Ev - 'ry hour I
bide, Or life is vain.
deed, Thou bless-ed Son!

I Need Thee Every Hour

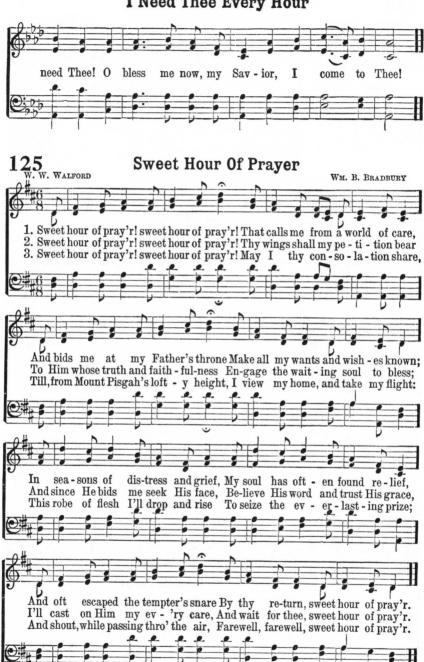

need Thee! O bless me now, my Sav - ior, I come to Thee!

125 Sweet Hour Of Prayer

W. W. WALFORD

WM. B. BRADBURY

1. Sweet hour of pray'r! sweet hour of pray'r! That calls me from a world of care,
2. Sweet hour of pray'r! sweet hour of pray'r! Thy wings shall my pe - ti - tion bear
3. Sweet hour of pray'r! sweet hour of pray'r! May I thy con - so - la - tion share,

And bids me at my Father's throne Make all my wants and wish - es known;
To Him whose truth and faith - ful-ness En-gage the wait - ing soul to bless;
Till, from Mount Pisgah's loft - y height, I view my home, and take my flight:

In sea - sons of dis-tress and grief, My soul has oft - en found re - lief,
And since He bids me seek His face, Be-lieve His word and trust His grace,
This robe of flesh I'll drop and rise To seize the ev - er - last - ing prize;

And oft escaped the tempter's snare By thy re-turn, sweet hour of pray'r.
I'll cast on Him my ev - 'ry care, And wait for thee, sweet hour of pray'r.
And shout, while passing thro' the air, Farewell, farewell, sweet hour of pray'r.

126 Savior, More Than Life

FANNY J. CROSBY

W. H. DOANE

1. Sav - ior, more than life to me, I am clinging, clinging close to Thee;
2. Thro' this changing world be - low, Lead me gen - tly, gen - tly as I go;
3. Let me love Thee more and more, Till this fleet - ing, fleet - ing life is o'er;

Let Thy pre-cious blood ap-plied, Keep me ev - er, ev - er near Thy side.
Trusting Thee, I can - not stray, I can nev - er, nev - er lose my way.
Till my soul is lost in love, In a brighter, brighter world a - bove.

D.S.—*May Thy ten - der love to me Bind me clo - ser, clo - ser, Lord, to Thee.*

REFRAIN

D. S.

Ev - 'ry day, ev - 'ry hour, Let me feel Thy cleansing pow'r;
Ev - 'ry day and hour, ev - 'ry day and hour,

127 Glory to His Name

Rev. E. A. HOFFMAN

Rev. J. H. STOCKTON

1. Down at the cross where my Sav - ior died, Down where for cleansing from
2. I am so won-drous-ly saved from sin, Je - sus so sweet-ly a -
3. Oh, pre-cious foun-tain that saves from sin, I am so glad I have
4. Come to this foun-tain so rich and sweet; Cast thy poor soul at the

Glory To His Name

sin I cried, There to my heart was the blood ap-plied; Glo-ry to His name.
bides with-in, There at the cross where He took me in; Glo-ry to His name.
en - tered in; There Jesus saves me and keeps me clean; Glo-ry to His name.
Sav-ior's feet; Plunge in to-day, and be made com-plete; Glo-ry to His name.

D. S.—*There to my heart was the blood ap-plied; Glo-ry to His name.*

CHORUS
D. S.

Glo - ry to His name,... Glo - ry to His name;...

128 Fifty-First Psalm

Slowly

1. From my sins hide Thou Thy face, Blot them out in Thy rich grace;
2. Freed from guilt, my tongue shall raise Songs Thy right-eous-ness to praise;
3. Sac - ri - fice or burnt of - f'ring Can to Thee no pleas-ure bring;

D. C.- Cast me not a - way from Thee, Nor Thy Spir - it take from me.
D. C.- Sac - ri - fice Thou wilt not take, Else would I the of - f'ring make.
D. C.- Thine ac - cept - ed sac - ri - fice, Thou, O God, wilt not de - spise.

D. C.

Free my heart, O God, from sin, Spir - it right re - new with - in.
O - pen Thou my lips, O Lord, Then my mouth shall praise ac - cord;
But a spir - it crushed for sin, Con-trite, bro - ken heart with - in.

129 The Twenty-Third Psalm

Arranged from Rev. WILLIAM H. HAVERGAL

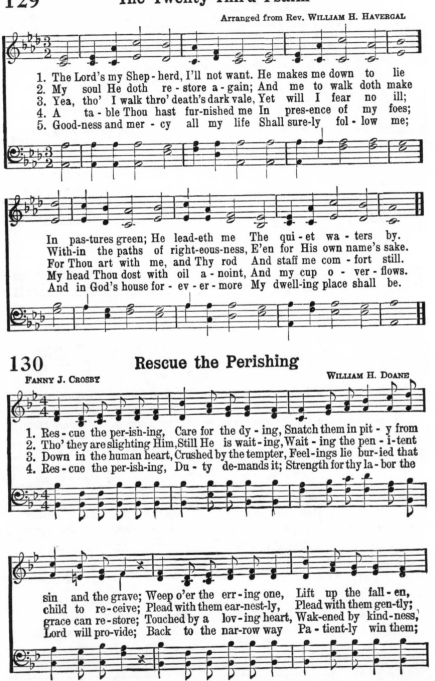

1. The Lord's my Shep-herd, I'll not want. He makes me down to lie
2. My soul He doth re-store a-gain; And me to walk doth make
3. Yea, tho' I walk thro' death's dark vale, Yet will I fear no ill;
4. A ta-ble Thou hast fur-nished me In pres-ence of my foes;
5. Good-ness and mer-cy all my life Shall sure-ly fol-low me;

In pas-tures green; He lead-eth me The qui-et wa-ters by.
With-in the paths of right-eous-ness, E'en for His own name's sake.
For Thou art with me, and Thy rod And staff me com-fort still.
My head Thou dost with oil a-noint, And my cup o-ver-flows.
And in God's house for-ev-er-more My dwell-ing place shall be.

130 Rescue the Perishing

FANNY J. CROSBY

WILLIAM H. DOANE

1. Res-cue the per-ish-ing, Care for the dy-ing, Snatch them in pit-y from
2. Tho' they are slighting Him, Still He is wait-ing, Wait-ing the pen-i-tent
3. Down in the human heart, Crushed by the tempter, Feel-ings lie bur-ied that
4. Res-cue the per-ish-ing, Du-ty de-mands it; Strength for thy la-bor the

sin and the grave; Weep o'er the err-ing one, Lift up the fall-en,
child to re-ceive; Plead with them ear-nest-ly, Plead with them gen-tly;
grace can re-store; Touched by a lov-ing heart, Wak-ened by kind-ness,
Lord will pro-vide; Back to the nar-row way Pa-tient-ly win them;

Rescue the Perishing

Tell them of Je - sus the might - y to save.
He will for-give if they on - ly be-lieve. Res-cue the per - ish-ing,
Chords that are bro-ken will vi-brate once more.
Tell the poor wan-d'rer a Sav - ior has died.

Care for the dy - ing; Je - sus is mer - ci - ful, Je - sus will save.

---

131 Footsteps of Jesus

MARY B. C. SLADE   A. B. EVERETT

1. Sweet-ly, Lord, have we heard Thee call - ing, Come, fol - low Me!
2. Tho' they lead o'er the cold, dark mountains, Seek - ing His sheep;
3. If they lead thro' the tem - ple ho - ly, Preach-ing the word;
4. Then at last, when on high He sees us, Our jour - ney done,

And we see where Thy foot-prints fall - ing Lead us to Thee.
Or a - long by Si - lo - am's foun-tains, Help - ing the weak:
Or in homes of the poor and low - ly, Serv - ing the Lord:
We will rest where the steps of Je - sus End at His throne.

D.S.—We will fol - low the steps of Je - sus wher - e'er they go.

CHORUS   D. S.

Foot - prints of Je - sus, that make the path - way glow;

132

The Old Time Religion

CHO.—'Tis the old time re-lig-ion, 'Tis the old time re-lig-ion,
1. It was good for our moth-ers, It was good for our moth-ers,
2. It has saved our ... fa-thers, It has saved our ... fa-thers,

'Tis the old time re-lig-ion, And it's good e-nough for me.
It was good for our moth-ers, And it's good e-nough for me.
It has saved our ... fa-thers, And it's good e-nough for me.

3. Makes me love everybody.
4. It was tried in the fiery furnace.
5. It was good for Paul and Silas.
6. It will do when I am dying.
7. It will take us all to heaven.

133

Take The Name Of Jesus With You

MRS. LYDIA BAXTER   W. H. DOANE

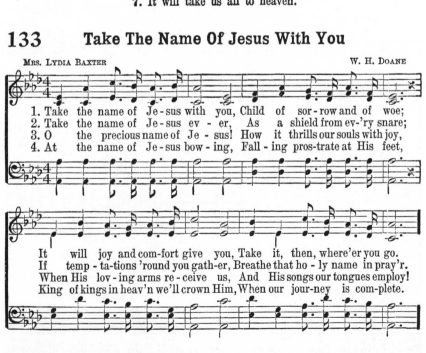

1. Take the name of Je-sus with you, Child of sor-row and of woe;
2. Take the name of Je-sus ev - er, As a shield from ev-'ry snare;
3. O the precious name of Je - sus! How it thrills our souls with joy,
4. At the name of Je-sus bow-ing, Fall-ing pros-trate at His feet,

It will joy and com-fort give you, Take it, then, where'er you go.
If temp - ta-tions 'round you gath-er, Breathe that ho - ly name in pray'r.
When His lov-ing arms re - ceive us, And His songs our tongues employ!
King of kings in heav'n we'll crown Him, When our jour-ney is com-plete.

Take The Name Of Jesus With You

CHORUS

Precious name, O how sweet! Hope of earth and joy of heav'n;

Precious name, O how sweet!

Precious name, O how sweet!... Hope of earth and joy of heav'n.

Precious name, O how sweet, how sweet!

134 Work, For the Night is Coming

Annie L. Coghill

Lowell Mason

1. Work, for the night is coming, Work thro' the morning hours; Work while the dew is
2. Work, for the night is coming, Work thro' the sun-ny noon; Fill brightest hours with
3. Work, for the night is coming, Under the sunset skies; While their bright tints are

sparkling, Work 'mid springing flow'rs; Work when the day grows brighter, Work in the
la - bor, Rest comes sure and soon. Give ev-'ry fly-ing min-ute Something to
glow-ing, Work, for daylight flies. Work till the last beam fad-eth, Fad-eth to

glow-ing sun; Work, for the night is com-ing, When man's work is done.
keep in store: Work, for the night is com-ing, When man works no more.
shine no more; Work while the night is dark'ning, When man's work is o'er.

135 Jesus is Mine

JANE C. BONAR
Chorus by I. B. W.

IRA B. WILSON

1. Fade, fade each earthly joy, Je-sus is mine! Break ev-'ry ten-der tie,
2. Tempt not my soul a-way, Je-sus is mine! Here would I ev-er stay,
3. Fare-well, ye dreams of night, Je-sus is mine! Lost is this dawn-ing light,
4. Fare-well, mor-tal-i-ty, Je-sus is mine! Wel-come e-ter-ni-ty,

Je-sus is mine! Dark is the wil-der-ness, Earth has no rest-ing-place;
Je-sus is mine! Per-ish-ing things of clay, Born but for one brief day,
Je-sus is mine! All that my soul has tried, Left but a dis-mal void;
Je-sus is mine! Wel-come, O loved and blest, Welcome, sweet scenes of rest,

Je-sus a-lone can bless, Je-sus is mine!
Pass from my heart a-way; Je-sus is mine!
Je-sus has sat-is-fied, Je-sus is mine!
Wel-come, my Savior's breast, Je-sus is mine!

CHORUS

Je-sus is mine! All else I

leave to fol-low Je-sus; Je-sus is mine; And I have naught beside, but Je-sus; His love can

nev-er fail, When doubts and fears as-sail, Thro' Him I shall pre-vail; Je-sus is mine.

136 The King's Highway

L. C. V.

L. C. VOKE

1. Trav-'ling on-ward to a cit-y bright and fair, Tears and sor-rows nev-er
2. There are man-y who are per-ish-ing to-day, Tread-ing not the straight and
3. "Go ye in-to all the world," the Sav-ior said, Tell of Christ—the joy-ful

en-ter there; Je-sus said He would a place pre-pare For
nar-row way; We must go to them with-out de-lay And
mes-sage spread; Je-sus suf-fered in the sin-ner's stead, Pre-

CHORUS

those in the King's High-way.
tell of the King's High-way. Walk-ing with Je-sus, by His
par-ing the King's High-way.

side I'll stay, Walk-ing with Je-sus in the nar-row way; Trav-el-ing a-

long to-geth-er day by day, Walk-ing in the King's High-way.

137 Deliverance Will Come

JOHN B. MATTHIAS

1. I saw a way-worn trav'ler In tat-tered garments clad, And, strug-gling
2. The sum-mer sun was shin-ing, The sweat was on his brow, His gar - ments
3. The songsters in the ar - bor That stood be-side the way At - tract - ed
4. I saw him in the eve-ning, The sun was bend-ing low, He'd o - ver-
5. While gazing on that cit - y, Just o'er that nar-row flood, A band of
6. I heard the song of tri-umph They sang up - on that shore, Saying,"Je-sus

up the mountain, It seemed that he was sad; His back was la - den heav-y, His
worn and dust-y, His step seemed very slow: But he kept pressing on-ward, For
his at - ten-tion, In - vit-ing his de - lay: His watchword being "Onward!" He
topped the mountain, And reached the vale below: He saw the golden cit - y, His
ho - ly an - gels Came from the throne of God: They bore him on their pinions Safe
has re-deemed us, To suf - fer nev-er-more." Then, casting his eyes backward On the

strength was almost gone, Yet he shouted as he journeyed,"De-liv-er-ance will come."
he was wending home, Still shout-ing as he journeyed,"De-liv-er-ance will come."
stopped his ears and ran, Still shout-ing as he journeyed,"De-liv-er-ance will come."
ev - er-last-ing home, And shout-ed loud,"Ho-san-na, De-liv-er-ance will come!"
o'er the dash-ing foam, And joined him in his triumph,—De-liv-er-ance has come!
race which he had run, He shout-ed loud,"Ho-san-na, De-liv-er-ance has come!"

REFRAIN

Then palms of vic - to - ry, crowns of glo - ry, Palms of vic - to - ry I shall wear.

138 Like a Mighty Sea

A. I. Zelley

H. L. Gilmour

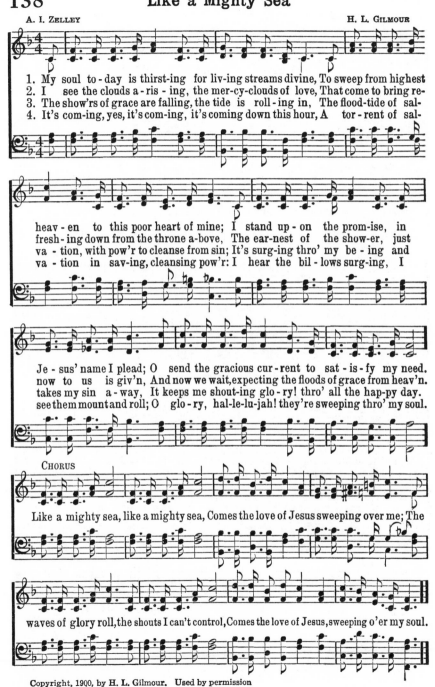

1. My soul to-day is thirst-ing for liv-ing streams divine, To sweep from highest
2. I see the clouds a-ris-ing, the mer-cy-clouds of love, That come to bring re-
3. The show'rs of grace are falling, the tide is roll-ing in, The flood-tide of sal-
4. It's com-ing, yes, it's com-ing, it's coming down this hour, A tor-rent of sal-

heav-en to this poor heart of mine; I stand up-on the prom-ise, in
fresh-ing down from the throne a-bove, The ear-nest of the show-er, just
va-tion, with pow'r to cleanse from sin; It's surg-ing thro' my be-ing and
va-tion in sav-ing, cleansing pow'r: I hear the bil-lows surg-ing, I

Je-sus' name I plead; O send the gracious cur-rent to sat-is-fy my need.
now to us is giv'n, And now we wait, expecting the floods of grace from heav'n.
takes my sin a-way, It keeps me shout-ing glo-ry! thro' all the hap-py day.
see them mount and roll; O glo-ry, hal-le-lu-jah! they're sweeping thro' my soul.

CHORUS

Like a mighty sea, like a mighty sea, Comes the love of Jesus sweeping over me; The

waves of glory roll, the shouts I can't control, Comes the love of Jesus, sweeping o'er my soul.

Copyright, 1900, by H. L. Gilmour. Used by permission

139 Awakening Chorus

CHARLOTTE G. HOMER · CHAS. H. GABRIEL

1. A - wake! a - wake! and sing the bless-ed sto - ry; A-
A-wake! a-wake!
2. Ring out! ring out! O bells of joy and glad-ness! Re-
Ring out! ring out!

wake! a - wake! and let your song of praise a - rise; A - wake! a-
A-wake! a-wake! A-wake!
peat, re - peat a - new the sto - ry o'er a-gain, Till all the
Re-peat, re-peat, Till all

wake! the earth is full of glo - ry, And light is beam - ing
a-wake! And light is beam-ing
earth shall lose its weight of sad-ness, And shout a - new the
the earth And shout a - new

MALE VOICES IN UNISON

from the ra-diant skies; The rocks and rills, the vales and hills re-sound with
glo - ri - ous re-frain; With an-gels in the heights sing of the great sal-

FULL HARMONY

glad - ness, All na - ture joins to sing the triumph song. The Lord Je-
va - tion He wrest - ed from the hand of sin and death.

Awakening Chorus

UNISON

ho - vah reigns and sin is back-ward hurled! Re - joice! re-
sin is back-ward hurled!

joice! lift heart and voice, Je - ho - vah reigns!

FULL HARMONY

Pro-claim His sov - 'reign pow'r to all the world, And let His
pow'r to all the world, And let His

glo - - rious ban-ner be un - furled! Je - ho - vah reigns!
grand and glo-rious ban - ner be un - furled! Je-ho-vah reigns! Je-ho-vah reigns!

Re - joice! re - joice! re - joice! Je - ho - vah reigns!
Re - joice! re - joice! re - joice!

140 The Victor's Song

J. V. R.

JAMES V. REID

f Introduction. Not fast

f Majestically

1. "Saved by grace," O let us sing the vic-tor's song, Lift-ing
2. "Saved by grace," a-gain take up the glad re-frain; Christ, the

heart and voice to join an-gel-ic throng; Christ in
Lord of lords, will reign on earth a-gain. Sor - row

Pow'r has con-quered sin's do - main, Through the
shall de-part from earth's op - pressed, No more

grave He went, and rose a - gain; Let us
groans shall rise from hearts dis - tressed; When on

The Victor's Song

rit.

tell the sto - ry Of His match-less glo - ry, Prais - ing
clouds descending, While all knees are bend-ing, He shall

ff CHORUS. *Stately.*

Christ, the Lamb for sin - ners slain. "Saved by
bring the na - tions in - to rest. "Saved by won-drous

grace!" O send the news to ev - 'ry na - tion; Christ, the
grace!" Tell them Christ, the might - y

Son of God, has died for all cre - a - tion; Praise Him, praise Him,
Son Let us

rit.

Give Him ad - o - ra - tion; Join ye all with glad ac-claim, Praise His great name.

141

I'm His Own

J. V. R.

JAMES V. REID

Introduction. Moderato

Not too fast

1. God is my Fa - ther, car - ing for me; I'm His
2. Ev - 'ry temp - ta - tion He helps to bear;
3. When by af - flic - tion I am op-pressed, Thro' His grace He

own; . . . Heir to a king-dom I am to be; I'm His
Ways of es-cape He's sure to pre-pare;
makes me His own; He whis-pers sweet-ly, "I'll give thee rest;" Thro' His grace He

own; . . . . He is pre - par - ing a home on high,
For ev - 'ry need there's a prom - ise true;
makes me His own; When thro' the val - ley of death I go,

Where there are man-sions be - yond the sky; There I shall dwell with Him
Strength for each day He will give a - new, And each dark hour He will
Je - sus will lead tho' dark wa - ters flow, And thro' e - ter - ni - ty's

I'm His Own

CHORUS *Joyfully*

bye and bye, I'm His own. . .
see me thro'; I'm His own. . . Joy - bells dai - ly are
years I'll know, I'm His own. . .

rit.

ring-ing with - in my hap - py heart; . . Sun - shine floods all my

be - ing and shad - ows de - part, For I'm liv - ing with Je - sus,

rit.

O how He keeps me with love un - - known. . . When He is
He keeps with match-less love un-known,

1 **2**

near there's noth-ing to fear, For I'm His own. . . own.

142 God Be With You

J. E. RANKIN   W. G. TOMER

1. God be with you till we meet a-gain; By His counsels guide, uphold you,
2. God be with you till we meet a-gain; 'Neath His wings protecting hide you,
3. God be with you till we meet a-gain; When life's perils thick confound you,
4. God be with you till we meet a-gain; Keep love's banner floating o'er you;

With   His sheep se-cure-ly fold you; God be with you till we meet a-gain.
Dai - ly man-na still pro-vide you; God be with you till we meet a-gain.
Put   His arms un-fail-ing round you; God be with you till we meet a-gain.
Smite death's threat'ning wave before you; God be with you till we meet a-gain.

CHORUS

Till we meet, ... till we meet,   Till we meet at Je-sus' feet;
Till we meet,   till we meet,   till we meet;

Till we meet, ... till we meet,   God be with you till we meet a-gain.
Till we meet,   till we meet,

INDEX

TOPICAL INDEX